P9-BYA-645

Escape to FREEDOM

By John H. Thielmann

© Copyright 1995 by John H. Thielmann
All Rights Reserved

John H. Thielmann
1084 Karen Way,
Mountain View, California 94040

ISBN 0-9646558-0-2
United States Library of Congress

Cover design by Graphics Plus
Los Altos, California

Printed by Patson's Press, Inc.
508 Tasman Drive, Sunnyvale, California 94089

Table of Contents

Table of Contents

Table of Contents

Upon the requests of my children and friends I ventured in writing my life experiences. The beginning of writing started with attending Mrs. Fanny Maud Evans' "Writer's Class" taught at the Los Altos adult education department. A used computer on loan from Mr. Bill Bradley facilitated the writing and Mr. Stefen Boyd taught me how to use the computer.

For the past two years I have been diligently at it. Mrs. Kay Gerrad corrected the manuscript and Mr. John Atwell proofread it. A hearty thank you to all that helped and encouraged me in this venture.

The final touches were made by my grandson, Major Dan Rose. He spent a considerable amount of time on this manuscript while being very busy, teaching others and preparing for his PhD exams.

Thank you all.

John H. Thielmann

Prologue
Escape To Freedom

The Bible tells us that the great eternal God of the universe has a grand plan governing the ages of time. It is a plan that has a purpose which, despite appearance often to the contrary, moves inexorably forward its grand conclusion.

Great events occur - kingdoms rise and fall, rulers are seated and deposed, wars, conflagrations, a plethora of natural disasters crash upon any given scene, but they are all played out before the backdrop of God's eternal plan and purpose which move on toward their inescapable climax.

This divine blueprint is not so much concerned with such events, though they do have their part to play in the total scheme. Its focus is more directed towards mankind.

Whether the great Creator is dealing with the total mass of humanity or with individual members of the human race, it would seem hardly possible not to see His hand intimately involved, whether acknowledged or ignored, in the affairs of men.

* * * * * *

John Thielmann's autobiography is an unusually poignant example of such intervention. It is a classic tale of immigrant escape in search of freedom from oppression. To us in the Western Hemisphere until more recent years, the story of immigrants coming to the New World has been in direction one from east to west. Mr. Thielmann's story is unique in that the direction of escape is from the west to east. His escape from Russia into China, his travel through Korea and Japan to the west Coast of the United States is a scenario filled with suspense and with repeated deliverance.

The word deliverance has been used advisedly. From the beginning of his long trek to the establishment of his new life in Reedley, California, John Thielmann's story is an illustration of what Solomon's words in his book of Proverbs portray when he says "...the path of the righteous is like the light of dawn, that shines brighter and brighter until the full day," Prov. 4:18.

Having entrusted his life into his Savior's care at an early age, John Thielmann experienced a continued unfolding of the protection, guidance, and grace in adversity anyone who has done likewise experiences in any given age. The events of his escape, his courtship and marriage, the years of provision at the Bible Institute of Los Angeles including his participation in the tour to raise funds for the Institute, his family's move to the San Francisco bay area - all give witness to the fact that God does make Himself responsible to keep the promises He has made to those, like John Thielmann, who have established a Father-son relationship with Him through faith in Jesus Christ.

It has been my privilege to know John Thielmann as a friend for the past several years. His story of the faithfulness of his Lord to him through these multiplied experiences has been a great blessing to me. My hope is that in like manner it will be an inspiration to all others who read this exciting saga.

John B. Atwell

June 13, 1994

Dear Dad:

Years ago I had asked you to write some of the stories you told us when we were little. Then as the years passed, I asked if you could tape a few stories so we wouldn't forget them.

I've enjoyed you telling us about your boyhood on the family farm in the Ukraine, where you were born. I was sad when you recounted the circumstances surrounding your father's death and you becoming head of the family when you were only 13 years of age. The incredible hardship you and your family experienced before and during the Bolshevik revolution and your subsequent escape from Communism and how your faith in God sustained you through all of this has been a marvel to me.

The incredible vacuum left in your life when Mom died was hard on all of us, but that became the catalyst for a new beginning for you. I enjoyed seeing you blossom after you started a writers class.

Your ancient typewriter became too cumbersome, so I asked if anyone in my Bible Study group had an extra computer they could loan you, sure enough one surfaced! Wonder of wonders, you've became quite proficient at having it do what you want it to.

You've come a long way, Dad! From horse and buggy to high tech, you have "hands on" experience.

Thank you for your life and legacy of faith!

Your loving daughter, Anna

Comments by Kay Gerrad

One man's fascinating journey through life no myth or fantasy needed. This autobiography is filled with adventure and uncertainty; yet there is an ever present dual thread of reliance on God and love of family.

I am privileged to know "Dad" Thielmann today, and can attest that these enduring qualities are extant in his life. John Thielmann is truly a man of faith and family.

Chapter 1

The Origin of the
Thielmann Family in Russia

I am writing this primarily for my family who encouraged me to capture these events on paper to preserve our heritage and the experiences which contributed to the shaping of all our lives. Though this story is primarily my experiences and recollections it is important for you to know the background of how my family came to be established in Russia which is where my personal story begins.

Early in the sixteenth century Menno Simons, a Dutch theologian, became a prominent leader in his community because of his outspoken faith and eloquent teaching ability for the gospel of Jesus Christ. In 1536, he joined a specific denomination of the Christian faith known as the Anabaptists, specifically known for practicing believers' baptism upon confession of faith, and stressing a life of discipleship and love as taught in the New Testament. Their interpretation of scripture, particularly about loving their enemies, produced strong convictions against participation in armed conflict for any reason. This strict belief in being conscientious objectors was a defining feature of their faith. Later they became known as Mennonites.

As a result of these significant religious differences, a great persecution broke out in Holland. Mennonites were hung, drowned, or dragged through the streets by horses while tied by their feet. They all fled from Holland to Germany. During the reign of Frederick the Great (17401786), these Mennonites were given religious freedom. However, for being exempted from military service, they had to pay an annual fee.

One of the tenants of the Mennonite faith was to work hard and, as a result, many became prominent businessmen and land owners. These newcomers became the envy of the local people, so they were forced to move to the less desired marsh lands and flooded areas. Making the best of their situation, they constructed dikes and drained the land. The sediments at the bottom of these long flooded areas proved to be extremely fertile and, once again, the Mennonites began to flourish by farming this rich land. The bountiful harvests again caused envy and the citizens complained to the King that he had given the Mennonites the best land! Forced to move once again, they went to the province of Danzig but longed to settle once and for all in a place less hostile to their ways and beliefs.

The vast steppes of the Ukraine, just conquered from the Turks by Russia, lay open for colonization. Catherine the Great made an offer to these "unwanted" people. If they would come and settle this vast land, they would be given many incentives. Among these were parcels of 175 acres of land, free transportation, religious freedom, ownership of their schools (taught in their own language), exemption from military duties, and self government among their own settlements. These privileges were guaranteed forever by a special imperial decree. However they were forbidden to proselyte among the native Russians.

A delegation was sent to confirm this offer and upon its return recommended acceptance. From 1789 to 1840, about 1,150 families, approximately 6,000 individuals, immigrated into Russia. One of these was a widow named Helena Thielmann.

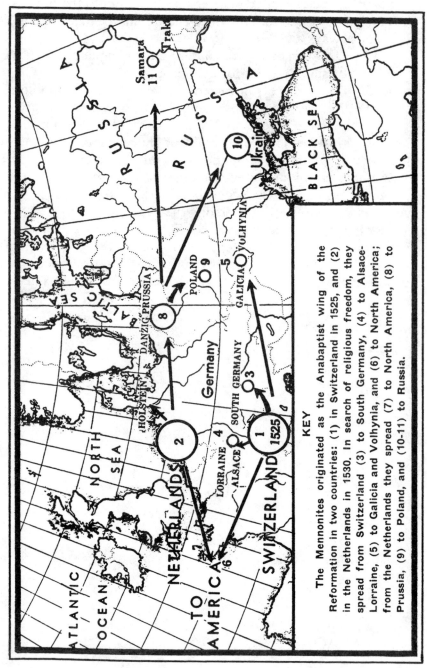

Origin and spread of the Mennonites

Chapter 2

The Origin of the Thielmann Family in Russia

In 1820 Helena Thielmann, with her three sons, Jacob, John, and Martin, arrived in the Molotschna settlement on the vast steppes of the fertile Ukraine. In the village of Neukirch, Helena's son, Jacob Thielmann, married Agatha Lettkemann in 1836. Jacob and Agatha's fourth child, John, born December 28, 1845, was my grandfather. The Russians had a tradition of giving the father's first name as the child's middle name regardless of the child's sex. All immigrants adopted this system, hence John's full name was John Jacob Thielmann.

Grandfather John J. Thielmann

When John was 12, his parents moved to Alexanderkrone, Molotschna, where they had acquired a farm of 65 dessiatine, or about 195 acres. When John completed his village school educa-

tion, he began training for blacksmithing and tooling. After ten years of training, he opened his own business in Lindenau and then in Schoenau, where he met Marie Loewen. They married in 1865.

In 1868, John and Marie decided to try farming, so they rented some land. After a successful trial period, they purchased a parcel of 180 acres near the village of Friedensfeld, in the province of Ekaterinoslaw. There John and Marie Thielmann began their family.

John J. Thielmann

They had six children while in Friedensfeld: John, Jacob, Maria, Henry, Helen, and Peter. In 1880, he rented a larger parcel of land consisting of 2898 acres.

The land he rented was a square plot. From the west it sloped gently downhill. It bottomed out with a sloped ravine, continued uphill, had a flat top and again continued gently downhill. A railroad ran through the upper flat land. It came in on a forty five degree angle from the northeast into this parcel, then ran north and south to the end of the land and turned southwest. A railroad station named Kudashewka, with pertinent buildings and a water tower, were located in the middle of this large rented parcel.

My Grandfather, John Jacob, moved with his family into a quickly constructed primitive dugout for a temporary living facility. This dugout was approximately one and a half miles from Kudashewka, and about a thousand yards from the ravine. Their seventh child, Johanna, was born here. My Grandmother died shortly after giving birth in 1885.

These primitive conditions caused other health hazards. The oldest son, John, woke up one night all wet. Thinking he had wet his bed, he woke his sister, Helena, and asked her to please give him some dry clothes. When she lit the lantern, she gasped! Her brother was blood soaked! A thirsty field rat had bitten him on the scalp and punctured a blood vessel in an attempt to get some moisture. In the morning they discovered the rat hole and plugged it up to prevent further incidents.

The owner of the land, a general's widow, approached John Jacob and asked him to buy her land. Since John Jacob didn't have the cash, she asked him to make his own terms. They made a contract to pay it off in ten years. During this time he made many improvements to the land. One improvement was building dams to section off the low areas. These dams created both a large and small body of water so they stocked them with fish. Because this fertile farm was so successful, he paid off the contract in only nine years.

The two to three feet of top soil, a black humus variety, produced excellent crops. The subsoil was red loam. John Jacob also discovered clay suitable for making brick. Now his dream of building a flour mill began taking shape. He constructed two brick kilns, which operated day and night, to produce the required quantity of bricks. All dwellings and barns were built out of these bricks.

The construction of a flour mill near the railroad, with living quarters for the children and employees, proved to be a convenient location to receive and ship products. They prospered for many years while their family grew.

Flour mill

Chapter 3

The Origin of the Thielmann Family in Russia

Wedding of my parents Henry and Sarah.

In 1906, Henry John, John Jacob's fourth son, my father, decided to marry. I asked my Grandma Unrau, on my mothers side, to tell me how my father met my mother and this is the story she told.

Grandma smiled and, after composing herself said, "One Sunday afternoon, John Jacob Thielmann and his son, Henry, drove up to my house in a horse drawn buggy. After greeting us he said, "My Henry wants to marry your Sara." That's how it happened! They were married February 2, 1906. I was born September 6, 1907, their firstborn.

I spent my childhood days in the two story building

Apartment where I was born.

Grandpa had built for his children. We occupied the southwest section, three rooms upstairs and a room downstairs. A separate building had a kitchen and sleeping quarters for a lady cook. The upstairs had a wide staircase leading to the entry. A door to the left connected the downstairs room. Two doors swung out, only one had a door handle so the other remained stationary. Outside was a balcony with three steps leading to the ground level. The kitchen was separated from the main house by about 25 feet. A wire from the upstairs to the bell in the kitchen served as signal to bring up the food. The windows were all alike. The tops were a semicircle and stationary. Only the lower section opened to the outside. Each room had one window with two sections. Both opened to the outside except the end room, which had two windows facing south and west. The ceilings were ten feet high. Two built in brick wall heaters, designed to burn coal, kept the house warm in the winter. The furniture, beds, tables and chairs, was simple. The pine floors were painted. A coat rack with a shelf, fastened to the partition wall at the head of the stairs in the center room, housed the family clock. Periodically, it needed to be wound. It chimed on the hour and on the half-hours day and night.

П. I. Тильманъ.

Peter J. Thielmann

The apartment complex had no plumbing; all water was hand carried. A sweet water well existed about 800 yards across the railroad tracks. This well supplied all domestic water. Father made a cabinet with a small tank for water with a spout on the bottom. Below the sink was a bucket that had to be periodically emptied. An outhouse served as the toilet. The electricity was supplied by the mill.

The steam engine of the flour mill required a large amount of water. A circular cement-lined pond, about 150 feet in diameter and 5 feet deep, had steeply sloped banks about 20 feet high. Where the bank met the pond, a four foot walkway was built all around. At the edge of one bank a tall power pole with an electric light on top served also as a pole to tie the clothesline to. A wooden trough near the pond was used to water the horses and cows. The water was pumped in from the small dammed lakes where Grandfather lived. My brother Henry was born in 1909 and Willy in 1911. My sister, Katja, was born in 1913. This wide open land with only a few buildings, far from any town, was the setting for many events that I can recall over my early years.

One such event happened in our home. Mother had forbidden us children to climb on the 24 inch wide, second story window sill. Willy, now two years of age, climbed onto the chair and then on the sill. It was spring time and everything was in bloom. As Willy stood there observing nature, mother came out of the bedroom. Seeing her child standing there, she hoped that the window was locked! It wasn't. She screamed his name, but at that moment his hand touched the glass, both windows opened to the outside, and the child tumbled out. Horrified, mother ran downstairs. She envisioned a horrible scene of her son's mangled and twisted body on the bricks below. As she ran around the corner, she saw Willy! He was just sitting and crying with some blood on his mouth and a few bruises on his body. Mother couldn't understand how a child falling 25 feet onto a brick sidewalk sustained only minor injuries. She believed the Lord had His hand in this miracle.

The whole business complex was operated by Jakob's three oldest sons and the sons-in-law. Each one had specific duties. Father was the buyer of required machinery and supplies. He traveled extensively to various countries including Germany. Close to Christmas time he would bring home mechanical toys. Because my curiosity about how they were put together was very great, I had to disassemble them! The only problem was that it was impossible for me to put them back together again!

Some machinery came one day. The crates were carried behind the housing complex but the nails had not been bent over for safety. I stepped on one and my mother worried about blood poisoning. It took weeks before it healed.

Chapter 4
Drowning

Below us lived father's younger brother, Peter, with his family. They had one boy, also named Peter, and two girls. Peter was about my brother Henry's age. They loved to play together. On one particular Monday, which was laundry day, the clothes-lines were tied to the power pole. Some lady had left the ropes excessively long so that they dragged on the ground. Both Henry and Peter amused themselves with the rope they discovered. First one was on the outside and the other on the inside running around the power pole until there was no more rope, like a may pole. Then they would switch and run the other way around. The details were not clear. Peter fell and rolled down the steep incline into the pond. Henry came running and told mother that Peter had fallen in the water! By the time mother and her sister-in-law had fished Peter out, he could not be revived.

It was a very sad experience for family when their only son had to die that way. Each time Aunt Helen saw my brother she would say, "Why didn't Henry drown instead of Peter?"

In the summer time the pond was in demand for all kinds of water sports. Weather permitting we were in the water nearly every day. Every kid knew how to swim. During winter, ice skating occupied our time. I admired the older cousins in their skilled maneuvers. We had fun. Our fun didn't last.

Chapter 5
Family Training

Most children I knew were related to me. My favorite cousins were the Peters' boys, Jacob, David, and Gerhard. Their family lived on the southeast end of the complex. As we were playing one summer day, I must have done something that angered all three of them. They threatened me. One against three, I surely could not win! In order to escape, I retreated to my "castle" and ran upstairs. In my haste, I forgot to lock the front door. Thinking I had escaped my pursuers, I was shocked when the doorknob twisted and all three stood in the doorway. Jacob had a long menacing pair of scissors, David held a huge butcher knife, and Gerhard was a supporting spectator. Jacob shouted, "Hans! Come down!" I refused. "Then we'll come up and murder you!" I was horrified! Jacob took a few steps. I wondered, "Now how do I defend myself?" Quickly I grabbed a chair and flung it down. It narrowly missed him, hit the entry floor, and broke a leg. Jacob started up again; I threw another chair down. Now I asked my brothers to hand me some more chairs. I was just ready to throw a third chair when the knob on the door turned and mother came in.

One look and mother assessed the whole situation. The three villains quickly retreated and ran home. She looked at the damaged chair, came up and then asked, "What are you up to?" "Mama, they wanted to murder me," I said. She went and got the rod, and did I get a spanking! Then she added, "What will Papa say about the broken chair?"

With much trepidation I waited now for father. Realizing his son already had his punishment, he asked me to fetch the chair and bring it to him. I was also asked to bring wires, pliers, nails and a hammer. First father lined the chair leg, wired it together neatly and then nailed it. He made the chair look nearly as good as new.

"Now son, this is your chair. Only you will sit on it," he said. My brothers stayed off of it. It was designated as my chair. Another type of punishment our family had was for the one being punished to stand in the corner until he repented. I did on that occasion. Next morning I met the previous day's enemies! We turned into friends again.

The last building to the west, behind our kitchen and on the south side of the road, was our schoolhouse. A one story brick building with a single entry in the middle facing south. On the right or east side were the living quarters for the teacher. On the left of the entry was a large room that housed benches for the students and as desk for the teacher. Windows were all around, in front two on each side of the entry. The sides each had two and the rear had four. The entry served both, the living quarters and the schoolroom. On the outside in the center of each window, pear trees were planted and trained in a peculiar shape. The trees were planted in the center of the window. The main trunk branched out, and grew a single branch horizontally to each side, and then turned vertical and went up the side of the window. In the fall the trees had fruit on them.

I asked my mother, "Who planted these trees and how did they make them grow like this?" She said, "I don't know, ask the teacher." He gave the same response, "I don't know." Those trees were really odd. A young fruit orchard of about three acres, consisting of a variety of trees, made the school look friendly and attractive. With anticipation I looked forward to my admission day at age six.

When I did go to school, my favorite subjects through the years were history, geography, mathematics, reading, and drawing with water colors. At home I was busy with my school assignments. Parents were somewhat relieved that there was less fighting between the children. The school work could not keep my mind from thinking of the trains passing our farm as they would blow their whistles.

The railroad activities, locomotives pulling box cars or open cars loaded with iron ore, always attracted our curiosity. Some engines would unhook several box cars and move them on the side tracks, to be unloaded at the elevator specifically built close to the tracks for this purpose.

Chapter 6
Family Training

In the summer, working men would spread out a large canvas, set up winnowing equipment, and winnow some of the grain not fit to be processed for flour. Being curious, I had to investigate any new machine. Even though the working men warned all the children to stay away from these large machines and their moving parts, these warnings weren't always heeded.

Somehow I managed to get too close to one machine, catching my hand in the gears. I screamed as loud as I could! Father heard and came running. My middle, ring, and small fingers were smashed. Father and I drove eighteen miles by horse and buggy to the nearest pharmacy where the druggist washed and dressed the injured fingers, saying he was not equipped to do more. The bone at the tip of the middle finger was crushed and grew together deformed. The other two fingers were thinner and fit in between the gears so only the upper and under muscles of these two were cut badly. They healed fairly well. During and after the harvest, farmers from distant villages delivered their crops, some with oxen and cart, others with horses. Their dogs also followed them. Uncle Jacob was in charge of receiving all the grain. Fortunately, some of his sons were able to relieve him from weighing the grain all day. He lived on the northeast end of the complex, occupying two floors because of his large family.

At the close of one particular day, after all the farmers had left, Uncle Jacob locked up the receiving section and was walking towards the office to have the receipts tabulated. To get to the office, located on the south end of the mill, he had to pass between the machine shop and the pond. Hearing a dog's wailing, he climbed the bank. He could see a white dog in the water up to his neck, standing on his hind legs. Jacob wanted to help.

He lowered himself to the walkway, grabbed the animal by the scruff of his neck, then pulled him out. The dog shook the water off his coat and kept running circles around Uncle while following him to his office. Jacob finished his business and then headed home. The dog, tail wagging, followed him to the door of his home. The children wanted to know why the dog was outside. The general opinion about this strange story was that maybe the dog became thirsty on this hot summer day. Finding no other water source than the pool, it attempted to lap some water and tumbled in. The children liked this dog and fed it, naming it Belka, which means 'Whitey' in Russian.

Months later, the real owner showed up again with a load of grain. Seeing his dog, he called it by name. The dog wagged its tail but would not approach its old master. The owner tried feeding it but still drew no response. Finally, we concluded the dog was abandoned and felt more allegiance to my uncle for saving and feeding it, than to its old master.

For the Mennonites, no work was performed on Sunday, either in business or on the farm. Since the main church was five miles away, the entire Thielmann clan gathered at grandfather's house for worship. The clan included a lot of people now.

Grandfather had remarried, a woman twenty years younger than himself, the oldest sister of his son-in-law, Jacob Wiebe. Her name was Katharine. They had eight children, the youngest two years older than I.

To accommodate the growing family, benches were set up in the front of the room for children; chairs were placed in the rear for adults. In the front of the room there was also a table where the speaker stood with his notes and the Bible. The service consisted mainly of reading from the Bible and notes from Spurgeon's sermon books. We kids enjoyed the singing but became restless and distracted others when the reading began. There must have been some discussion about this because from then on, the children stayed home on Sundays.

Death In The Family

Grandfather's health began to fail and he suffered a stroke. February 19, 1912, he passed away. They buried him about three hundred yards southeast of the house in the wooded area. This area became the burial plot for the whole family. A monument made of beautiful granite stone decorated his grave. The estate, land, and property was already divided while Grandfather was alive. Some of his children started their own buildings while some were content where they lived.

Chapter 7
Russia at War with Germany

The year 1914 started out ominously with fearful expectations and threats of war with Germany. A general mobilization of able-bodied men let us know we were at war. Early in the summer, we had a complete solar eclipse in our area. The Russian people, who were superstitious, anticipated disaster. The declaration of war on Germany disturbed us all. The government forbid us to speak the German language, our native tongue; this ban included the school. Along with other private citizens, our community baked large quantities of bread and shipped them to the army. Our estate contributed about five hundred horses to the Czar's war efforts. Many of our workers were drafted and a shortage of help threatened to shutdown the mill.

Father upper left - Red Cross

Father was drafted but was able to serve as a medic in the Red Cross as an alternative to the army. He left home to ferry wounded from the front to the interior hospitals. Quite frequently these trains would pass our station. Mother wanted us to watch for train number one-ninety-six, the one father served on. Father made a satisfactory arrangement with his commanding officer. Whenever he passed our station, he could get off to visit us. With the next passenger train, he then caught up with the Red Cross party. Prisoners of war started to arrive, mostly Austrians and Hungarians, with an occasional Pole. Ten Austrian prisoners with one officer were assigned to substitute for workers in our mill who were drafted. The war did not stop my studies though.

I learned reading and writing quickly, both in German and Russian. Books like, "Pilgrim's Progress," and, "Uncle Tom's Cabin," fascinated me and helped me develop a new dimension-moral reasoning. Other books started being widely distributed as well. War books began arriving, praising the gallantry of the Russian Cossacks and the accuracy of their artillery.

When the war casualties increased substantially, the local hospitals were filled and the deliveries of wounded were changed to areas where space was available. Mother felt insecure and needed a companion to stay with us. Her mother, Grandmother Unrau, lived in Siberia. After Grandpa's passing, Grandma moved to Siberia to live with her children. The decision was made for her to stay with us.

Chapter 8
Grandma Our Sunshine

That summer, we all pitched in and dried a lot of apples, pears, and cherries. Determined to take some along for relatives, Mother left for Siberia. Grandma agreed to come on the condition that two orphans she took care of, a boy and a girl, children of her deceased son, would come along. Grandma compromised, allowing the boy to stay with one of the uncles. The girl came along. Grandma had a grim fate most of the time. After Grandpa died, she stayed with one of her children for a few months then moved to the next child's home. This was her routine year after year. She welcomed the chance to stay with her youngest daughter, my mother. Only once had I seen Grandpa and Grandma Unrau when they lived in our neighborhood.

I remember when visiting them, we children slept in the living room under a large wall clock. The loud ticktock and chimes kept me from sleeping. In the morning I complained that the clock kept me from resting.

The permanency of Grandma's stay was a very welcome experience. Everything changed. She knew many stories and we appreciated the daily Bible reading. In many ways Grandma made herself useful in knitting, darning socks, and mending clothes. She also kept discipline in the house. House duties kept the slightly older cousin Agnes, preoccupied. Besides, boys did not play with girls!

Conversations inside the house and in general, was carried on in Dutch. Reading the Bible and praying was done in German. Since it was prohibited to use the German language in school, Russian was a good substitute. Farmers delivering their products to be milled spoke the Ukrainian language. Most of the hired help were Ukrainians. It was just natural to pick up these languages and posed no problem. It was during one of these conversations with the Ukrainians that I heard some interesting news.

War rumors were circulating that Germany was using lighter-than-air flying machines. These Zeppelins, as they were called, were able to fly long distances. They could moor and tie to any high object. Later a complaint was brought before the government concerning potential collaboration with the

Germans. A high observation tower, about 90 feet tall, built for the purpose of ventilating fruit cellars on our estate, came under scrutiny and was ordered to be torn down. The tall smoke-stack at the flour mill met with the

Estate with tower.

same fate. It was torn dawn below the roof level. The gendarmery feared that the Zeppelins were flying in regularly at night. Because we were of German origin, they assumed we could be transmitting sensitive information to the Germans. There, of course, was absolutely no truth to these allegations. Fortunately nothing ever came of these allegations.

Father had not been home for some time. Because of the many war casualties, trains had to make shorter trips. Dad had written for mother to meet him near Poltava. Taking me along as an escort, Mother asked me to watch for every train number. Being positioned near the window, I gazed out over the passing scenery. Occasional villages, clumps of trees or a grazing cow would come into view. Then an opposite train rushing by would block the view. Mother then asked, "You see any number on it?" There was no number on it. Another train passed with large crosses and numbers marked on each side for identification. Shortly behind this one came another train into view. "Mama, look! Number 196 marked on the side!" I shouted. She looked and sure enough, it was the train father was on. We then realized father would not be meeting us! What next? After a while she said,

Distant view of estate and business.

"We have relatives here, the Dicks." Since it was Sunday, we got off and visited.

Mr Dick, an accomplished musician, was also an owner in a flour mill business with his relatives. I recognized him and felt at home. His children were somewhat older, but entertaining, and the day passed quickly. We arrived home safely. To Grandma, Mother expressed disappointment about the entire trip.

Grandma gave life a different, more stable, dimension. Whenever Father was at home, Scripture and prayers were read and observed at breakfast. Grandma was a spiritual and physical fortress, especially in Father's absence. At a specific time of the day, she would call us together and read from the Bible. The stories were fascinating, and the prayers impressive. Her hands were always busy, either knitting, mending or darning socks. Any question I had, Grandma had the answer. She was like a walking encyclopedia to me.

Grandma Katherine Thielmann lived in the lower apartment next to us. Quite often it happened that when we played outside, Grandma would come out. I would greet her. She then would say in a sarcastic tone, "Why doesn't your dad come and visit me?" or "Nobody ever visits me." I had no answer.

Talking with Grandma Unrau, who lived with us, I addressed this problem to her, "Why is Grandma Thielmann sarcastic?" She was quiet for a little while and then said, "We ought to love and pray for her." I learned the lesson to differentiate between a person's character and their personality idiosyncrasies and then decide which ones to emulate.

Chapter 9

The Revolution

The war had a very grim outcome once the entire Russian front collapsed. Father came home, took off his uniform and was a civilian again. Workers, who survived, reappeared. It seemed as if there was a standstill in all business activity and social activity outside our community. A state of anarchy existed. The prisoners of war working at the mill packed up and went home. There were no regular train movements. Individual engines arrived loaded with men equipped with all kinds of weapons, waving black flags. They called this a revolution.

Our parents must have anticipated problems living near the railroad because we promptly moved to the estate which was farther away from the station. We barely settled into our new environment when Russian peasants from all directions appeared and, without asking permission, started to steal horses, cows, wagons and farm equipment from our property. We were all bewildered as to where this would lead. Previously friendly farmers suddenly turned out to be greedy and hauled away anything they wanted. Our convictions about not using violence against anyone was followed to the best of our ability. We did not resist.

Chapter 10
German Troops Invade the Ukraine

Summertime had come and the harvest was in full swing. We got along the best we could with the remaining horses and equipment. Then, German and Austrian soldiers with war equipment appeared. Father explained that the invasion by the Germans into the Ukraine was for the purpose of supplying food for the troops still in Germany. Empty railroad cars were rounded up and the remaining wheat and other grains were confiscated and sent off to Germany.

Whole divisions of German soldiers moved in to our area but we did not resist. The soldiers ordered every Russian village, whose citizens participated in looting, to return the taken items and animals by a certain date, or face reprisals. Father, a hired hand, and I went to the closest village to reclaim what was ours. We spotted three of our horses. One had a broken neck or at least he could not raise his head. We asked the man holding this particular animal what happened. He replied that the animal had fallen. Father would not reclaim the injured animal and for humane reasons asked the man to destroy the horse.

We were able to claim some cows as well as the two horses. They walked with a much slower pace so Father suggested the hired hand and I each take a horse and ride home ahead of him. To cover the remaining eighteen miles normally would take at least two hours. The sun was setting behind threatening clouds so we started out with a trotting pace for about an hour. A heavy rain overtook us and the horses slowed down to a walk. Wet and chilled, we arrived home past midnight. Next day I had a fever and stayed in bed. Pain in the middle of my back turned out to be the beginning of a huge boil which took over a month to fully heal.

Chapter 11
Prayers Tested and Proven

Many transport trains of grain had gone west. One day a train was sabotaged. A group of young men from a nearby village were implicated for perpetrating this act of terrorism against the Germans. A division of German troops surrounded the village. Not having a translator, the general showed up at Uncle John's house. He explained what happened and that the villains were followed to this village. He wanted Uncle to translate their demands to hand over the two hundred young of the village or face annihilation.

The village had eighteen thousand inhabitants. All houses were built of sod brick or mud and covered with straw roofs. If fire ever got started up wind, it would sweep through the entire settlement in no time. Many of the older men knew my uncle. Some had worked for him and he had done business with many others. He went along to translate the demand and ultimatum for the Germans. The villagers had twenty-four hours to comply or face complete annihilation. Artillery and machine guns were strategically placed surrounded the village. Uncle reasoned with the elders of the village who told him their young men were not there.

As soon as my uncle came back, he approached my parents and Grandma. He asked that we please pray for this situation that God would intervene to save the village. Grandma came outside and asked us children to pray about this very dangerous and volatile situation.

Twenty-four hours expired. The Germans again summoned Uncle to warn the people in the village of the very critical situation. He talked to the general explaining that, because we were a German speaking people, we were at a high risk of being seen as collaborators with the Germans especially since he was translating for them. We prayed. On the third day the division pulled out and left. The Lord had quickly answered our prayers!

Chapter 12
Anarchy

Late in September of 1917 the western front collapsed. The Allied forces prevailed. All German and Austrian troops were recalled. The retreating German armies compelled some farmers from the next Mennonite settlement to furnish transportation. Six wagons with Mennonite drivers were singled out to haul troops approximately fifty miles. For several days the drivers failed to show up back at their settlement.

Scouting parties went out to locate the missing drivers. They found the place where the entire column was ambushed and annihilated. The drivers they found separately, in kneeling positions, cut to pieces with sabers. Since the bodies were in a state of decomposition, they were placed in hastily constructed caskets and deodorant was poured over the boxes. Closed casket ceremonies were performed. My parents went to this very sad funeral. The notorious bandit and henchman, Makchnow, organized a large group of insurrectionists. They were armed to the teeth, did not observe any law, and were not responsible to any authority. The country was without a government. This outlaw organization now terrorized the people of the southern Ukraine. Machnow openly vowed to destroy all German speaking people; his group had massacred the drivers. After the funeral I noticed my parents expressions. Father's face had an ashen appearance. Mother's was drawn. For quite some time neither spoke. Then they remarked that it was a very sad funeral.

All of us on the estate were apprehensive about the future. A few days later, a rumor spread that all the Thielmanns would be destroyed that night. The whole clan, late that evening, assembled in the two story building near the railroad. Everyone piled into the upper story and laid on the floor in the dark, making no noise. The men stationed themselves at strategic places. Everyone knew the signals if anyone approached from the outside.

We lay crowded on the floor. Henry lay next to me. At midnight he suddenly cried loudly. I tried to quiet him while he whimpered about his knee. Someone trying to move in the darkness stepped on his leg and dislocated the knee. There was no outside disturbance that night. Everyone went home. Henry was taken to a bone specialist but received no relief from the pain. However, while playing that afternoon, he had been sitting cross-legged. Suddenly, he jumped up and said, "It doesn't hurt any more!" We children slept in a very narrow room. Bunk beds were set up for two of us. I elected to sleep on top. Willy had his own. A few days later, at dusk, I woke up from the noise of the front door slamming. It was so loud that I ventured down to investigate. Walking through my parents' bedroom, I saw their beds were empty! Proceeding to the outside door, I wondered what happened. Meanwhile, my brothers got up and were behind me. The three of us stood in our night clothes wondering what to expect next.

Suddenly mother's face appeared through the window and she quietly let herself in the house. When she saw us standing there, she fell down on her knees, embracing us all. In a sobbing voice she repeatedly exclaimed, "Children, forgive me for having forsaken you." Suddenly Dad stood behind her also looking very upset.

The previous day, they had received news of another threatening rumor. Fear had gotten the best of them and after dark they had run out of the house and hidden behind the lake in the field. They huddled together, staying there until dawn, before venturing back again. They reasoned that the bandits probably would not harm children. Mother promised never to leave us again.

Troublesome days lay ahead. The bandits found it more profitable to organize in smaller groups. Every civilian feared these ruthless men. But our farming had to continue so to increase security we worked during daylight only. Business went on as usual, in spite of harassment.

About eleven o'clock one early summer morning, a band of about ten armed men appeared. "Where is the boss?" their leader shouted. Father identified himself. "Where is your gold and silver?" Evidently the reply did not come fast enough. A pistol was thrust into fathers mouth and he was pinned to the wall with his hands up in the air. I stood about twelve feet away. These men seemed short tempered. Dad gagged and the gun was removed. Father then ordered someone to go into the cellar after describing the location of the treasure box. When it was brought up, the men grabbed it and then demanded lunch. While mother and the girls busied themselves to prepare the food, the band disappeared. I breathed a sigh of relief Thanking God that no one was killed or injured. Armored trains with regular troops started to appear. The small bands disbanded! Unfortunately, as soon as the troops were gone, the bandits reappeared.

Chapter 13
The Epidemic

In late September 1919, some of these bands appeared demanding to be housed and fed. About thirty men crammed into our little apartment. The back bedroom was vacated and, because we did not have adequate bedding, straw was hauled in for them to sleep on. Because of the unsanitary living habits of these men, typhoid fever spread and rapidly took a heavy toll. One of the men took seriously ill. Dad told the bandits the man had all the symptoms of the dreaded disease. Scared, the men packed up and left, taking the ill person with them, presumably to get better medical treatment somewhere else. Scarcely a week went by without one or two funerals. It continued all summer and into the fall. Father's next older brother, Jacob, with a wife and two children, a boy and girl, lived next door. They all took sick. No one wanted to take care of them for fear of getting sick themselves. At breakfast time a few days later Mom and Dad had a discussion. Dad said, "There is no one that wants to take care of Jake and his family. I will have to do it."

"But what if you get sick?" Mother asked. "How could I take care of this family?"

"But he is my brother," Dad replied. "I will be careful." Without delay he set up a large kettle, holding about twenty or more gallons of water, outside the ill family's apartment. A wood fire brought the water to a boil. Dad went inside, pulled the soiled linen out from each one, and dumped them into the boiling kettle. This he did day after day, until his brother and family recovered.

The Darkness

Early in December, Dad took sick. Mother now took care of him. At mealtime we would enquire about Dad's condition. In a few words she would tell us that he is very ill. Since we had no doctors, a pharmacist was brought in. He discovered a boil inside dad's throat. With an instrument he punctured it. In a few words he told mom that it was all he could do.

On December 27, 1920, late at night, mother woke us children and said, "Come and see Papa before he dies." I approached his bed as he exhaled for the last time. Five chairs were standing on the west wall. Mother sobbed when Grandma came in. She suggested that we kneel and pray. Grandma prayed a very comforting prayer and we children followed. After we were seated, Mother exclaimed, "What can I do now? I do not know anything about the business." Grandma comfortingly said that the Lord never forsakes His own and that He takes care of the widows and the orphans. Having calmed down, Mother exclaimed, "John, you are the

Widowed mother and children.

oldest. Take care of what has to be done; I depend on you." Mother was about six months along in her pregnancy and couldn't help lift Father. Men carried the body wrapped in a white sheet, to the carpenter shop, and laid him on a bench. A casket was soon prepared.

The following day I suggested to my brothers, "Let's go and view Daddy's body." I had the key in my hand, so they followed. We stood there looking at the body in the casket. No one said a word. Curiosity got the best of me so I reached in and touched his forehead. It was ice cold. Quietly we all walked home. My thoughts were preoccupied about how life ends this side of eternity. With pick and bar, the grave was dug through the frozen ground close to Grandpa's grave. A few relatives and the minister from the nearby church appeared. After the burial, Mother and the children were the last ones to leave. "Farewell, Daddy!"

At home, Mother said she did not feel too well. Going to bed, she remarked,"I hope not to get the disease father had." She did. After three weeks, she regained consciousness. No sooner was she on her way to recovery when she came down with small pox. Getting over this hump, birth contractions started. With horse and buggy, I went five miles to fetch the midwife. I had no answer for many of the questions the midwife asked. Mother gave birth to a girl who we named, Sarah.

A few months after birth, little Sarah was very restless past midnight. The darkness usually had not bothered Mother in feeding the baby. This night after feeding the baby, she reached over the railing, thinking she was at the edge of the crib and let her free-fall to her bed. Instead she had overreached and dropped the child on the floor. The sudden cry of the child and mother's hasty call for light woke us all. Sarah didn't survive this accident. She was buried next to father's grave.

Chapter 14
New Management

Tim, a prisoner of war from Poland, had worked for father ever since we moved. He had refused to go back as it was worse in Poland. Being single, he had no attraction to return. We considered him as our foreman. Good qualities were in his character but also a very dangerous one. When he got angry, he would go into a rage almost beyond control. Ordinarily he would curse and swear, but not when I was around. Mother had informed him that I was the boss. He respected me.

Not having too much knowledge of agriculture, I needed training. At dawn Tim would come and knock on my bedroom window, and tell me it was time to get up. After dressing, I would make the rounds to inspect the work being performed. On one particular day, Tim woke me. When I was almost dressed, he returned and excitedly blurted, "All the horses from the barn are gone!" The previous night the barn had been securely locked. This morning the doors were open. I ran and looked around stunned by this unexpected event. Only one mare that had foaled the previous night was left by the thieves.

Very disturbed, I brought the sad news to Mother, who was still convalescing. Dismayed, she sat up in bed and asked what we were going to do? After awhile a suggestion was made to go to the uncles and ask them to loan us one horse. That would help us do at least some of the spring seeding.

Heavy hearted, I walked first to Uncle Jacob. Explaining the situation to him, he refused saying, "I need them all myself now." The other two uncles had the same answer. Mother could not comprehend why all this calamity had hit us. Consulting with Tim about this dilemma, he made the suggestion that we break in a cow and team her together with the mare. We tried teaming the two different animals. The cow had a slower pace and chased flies with its head. This scared the horse which was afraid of the cow's horns. Each time, the horse bolted to the side. My brother and I each had to guide an animal. Not too long after this my uncles came and prepared some of our land for the next years seed time after their crop were in.

Chapter 15
New Light

The horrors of the past, and the loss of Father and many relatives, made the future look dark. But despite these times of trial nature had unfolded its spring beauty for Easter. Agnes, an older cousin by five years, had invited all the children into the meadows for a Sunday school gathering. We all squatted down with expectation and waited. Eloquently, Agnes explained Easter and the Resurrection. From Scripture, she proved that we all were in need of a Savior. It was a reasonable explanation. My brother and I responded by accepting Jesus as our Lord and Savior. This is the place and time of my conversion.

Under Grandma's guidance, I started to pray and read the Bible systematically. Next, we presented ourselves as candidates for membership to the church. We were first baptized, then accepted as members.

Often I visited Father's grave site and lay down in the grass and meditated. The question came to mind whether all these tragedies could have been prevented. As a ten year old boy, soon after Father had come home from the war front and we had moved to the estate, I plagued him with the request to move to America. "We are getting a raw deal here in Russia," I would say. He then put the question to me, "Would you want to learn the English language?" When I said yes, he told me to go and see Uncle Abe. One morning after finishing breakfast, I ran to the barn and requested a gentle mare. Bareback, I rode the one mile to Uncle Abe's home. In a friendly manner, he listened to my request to teach me the English language. He asked me if Dad already had applied for exit visas. I said no. He told me to come back when we got them. He died before father by about six months.

1921 was a dry year. Tragically, the spring crops didn't grow and only some of the winter wheat seasoned. The severity of this situation prevailed over all of Southern Russia. The subsequent famine caused more fatalities than the disease we had lived through. The civil war, lack of transportation, and looting caused great shortages in a number of vital products. Instead of coal oil lamps, we used animal fat in a dish with a wick in it. Grandma produced silkworm eggs from an unknown source. At the beginning of spring, she waited until the mulberry trees put out their leaves. Then, the sheet with eggs was spread inside the window sill, since the sun caused the hatching. After about forty days the worms spun cocoons the size, shape, and look of a large peanut shell. Once the worms finished spinning the cocoons, the cocoons were gathered into sacks and baked in the bread oven. Next, a small amount of the cocoons were dumped into hot soapy water. The silk now separated easily and the pupa was removed and dried. My remarkable Grandma then spun thread and knitted stockings for all of us. They seemed to never wear out, but did have one drawback, they were not warm. Father anticipated some of these shortages. Shoes were made with wooden soles; the tops were made from animal hide. Planting linseed, we now had flax for linen. A hired woman spun fine thread in the wintertime and rolled the thread into balls. A local weaver made linen in bolts of one and a half feet by one hundred feet. We rolled the bolts out on the grass, poured water on them, then let the sun do the bleaching. Mother knew how to sew pants, shirts and skirts for the girls. A substitute for sugar was honey or cooked molasses from melons or watermelons. We were thankful Father had such great foresight.

The summer before Father died, he went to the next village to obtain five beehives. Late that night, he came home very distressed. Because he unloaded the hives in a hurry, they were not set properly. So, he told my brother and I to get up before dawn to reposition the hives. The next morning we did as ordered. However, one hive was in a hollowed out tree trunk about twelve inches in diameter. As we tried moving it, bees came out of the stump by the dozens. Dropping it roughly, we shied away until the bees calmed down.

At this time, an an elderly man about eighty years of age, possibly five feet tall, with long, large hands, came up the road. Surprised, he asked, "What are you doing here this early?" I said we were going to reset the bee hive but were afraid of being stung. He volunteered to do it for us. He walked up and grabbed the stump, raised it off the ground, and carried it barely a foot. The disturbed bees swarmed out, covering his head, face and beard. When he dropped the stump, more bees came out. Since the lake was only a hundred feet away he ran as fast as he could to the water, jumped in, and ducked under.

It looked so funny we couldn't help but laugh! Although we were but a few feet away, the disturbed insects did not touch us. The man, while holding his breath under water, scrubbed his face and the bees would float. But the moment he poked out his head, the swarm came on him with a renewed attack. He repeated this several times before the attack abated. I can't remember a time when we laughed so hard at such a spectacle. I would have paid money to see such a show but it was free!

His long boots, which reached above his knees, were filled with water when he finally climbed out. Seeing us laughing, he swore and cursed to no end. (I later made an interesting observation. While running to the water, he prayed; coming out of it, he swore.) Father always took care of that hive, by being adequately covered with protective netting and prepared to calm the insects with smoke.

Honey was new to us and we loved it. After Dad died, Mother wanted to take up where he left off. Following the hibernation of the bees in the cellar during the winter, we set them out in spring. Everything was blooming; the bees were gathering the nectar. Mother decided to peek into the hives. She asked me to come along and hold the smoker. We thought we were prepared for an attack, but she had overlooked putting on pants.

Four of the hives were gentle insects; the ones that were in the stump, looked different. They had a darker color and stubby bodies. This was a Caucasian breed. Dad had transferred them into a regular hive. As soon as the lid was removed, the swarm started to buzz. I encouraged Mother to use more smoke. I had no protection and didn't dare come closer. The pesky bees found a way to get under Mother's skirt. The poor woman panicked and dropped everything, which caused more trouble. Running from the hives, she took off her headgear and all her clothes. I was ashamed to look in the direction Mother had retreated. After about ten minutes, she summoned me to gather her clothes and bring them to the bush where she huddled. When she had dressed, she came and said, "John, I do not care what happens to those creatures. If you want them, you take care of them." I did, and we had plenty of honey to substitute for sugar.

Chapter 16
Harassments

Unfortunately, perilous times were not over! Unexpected soldiers appeared all hours of the day. For example, late in August, upon finishing lunch, my brother and I decided we wanted to have some melon. Excusing ourselves, we walked to the melon patch located about 300 yards uphill on the road. Looking for a ripe melon, I noticed two horsemen riding into the backyard. Paying no significant attention, we kept on eating our fruit. Suddenly, I saw Mother running, looking in both directions. Never before had I observed her running like that. She must not have seen us, for arriving at the clump of tall and tight growing weeds, she fell to her knees and ducked down. With folded hands and moving lips, she prayed. I knew something was wrong. As I came closer, she looked in my direction putting her finger to her lips, which meant silence.

From around the house came one of the riders with a hand gun in his left hand and a drawn saber in his right. Staggering from side to side, it was apparent he was intoxicated. As he came closer, I could hear him cursing and muttering, "Where is she?" Seeing us boys standing there, he stopped and after looking around went back. After about fifteen minutes they both departed. Their leaving without molesting anyone was a wonderful relief and answer to prayer!

Even in the midst of severe shortages, the inventive mind Grandma possessed profited our kitchen supply with vegetable oils and molasses. Acres of pumpkins, beets, melons and watermelons were planted. The cattle devoured items we didn't consume. The seed from all of these varieties were separately dried and sacked. Together with the sunflower seeds, we took them to a crudely constructed oil pressing plant. The seeds were machine peeled, winnowed, ground, fried and pressed. Each customer took his turn. The bystanders asked us how we could gather all these seeds. Need is the mother of invention!

To get molasses out of melons and watermelons, the fruit was cut in half, the juice pressed out and the seed removed and dried. To do this, we nailed together a large wooden frame out of 2" x 8" x 3' x 6'. The bottom was covered with thin gauged flat metal. This served as an evaporating container. It was set on several layers of brick to keep it off the ground and to allow fire under it. Evaporation of water helped thicken the content to molasses, which we then put up in containers.

Chapter 17
The New Order

By 1922 the new government had its iron hand everywhere. A new order came out cancelling all private ownership of any land, business or buildings. No one had the right to employ another person. We had to dismiss all hired help except Tim, who did not want to leave.

That year we had a fair crop. An announcement was issued by the government stating that a commission would come to assess how much of the harvested crop a farmer could retain. The rest would be confiscated. Our original agreement with the government was being slowly broken and this scared us all.

While threshing the wheat crop, Tim approached me and quietly talking so no one would overhear. He had a plan to help us save some of the crop from confiscation. He said, "Around midnight I will come and wake you. Be sure not to disturb anyone. I need your help to sack some wheat, and guide me to the barn from the warehouse. The whole operation is going to be conducted in total darkness."

We went and familiarized ourselves with the path we would take, a distance of about 450 yards. With keys in hand, he opened the doors of the warehouse. I familiarized myself with the location of the shovel and sacks we would need.

Using the excuse of being extremely tired from having worked extra hard that day, I went to bed with my clothes on. At the appointed time, I heard his voice softly calling. Noiselessly we walked the distance to the barn. Once inside the building, knowing exactly where the sacks lay, I held one up and Tim shoveled the wheat in.

Normally we would tie the end but this took extra time so we skipped this step. A full sack contained about 40 kilograms. Tim knelt down, gathered the end of the sack and I helped him lift it off the floor. He dumped them near a high opening in the rear of the barn. He planned to cover the pile of bags with hay in the morning. All had been planned with a wagon load of feed the day before. In haste we covered the grain with this feed. We walked this distance nine times. Already very tired and since it seemed it was getting somewhat lighter, Tim whispered we would do only one more sack. Filled and loaded, I locked up the barn doors. We were opposite Uncle Jacob's apartment, Tim slipped and the sack opened spilling a large portion of the grain. The noise caused dogs to bark. I helped Tim load what was left in the sack, back on his shoulder and off we ran. Quite a lot was spilled on the ground. Tim went to the barn and I to my room.

What seemed like only a few minutes later, Uncle Jacob came knocking on my door. With an excited voice Uncle remarked about the spilled wheat on the road in front of his apartment. I went with him to look. In the meantime, a large flock of chickens had happened upon the grain and were busy cleaning up this tell tale spill. In no time it was all cleaned up. Praise the Lord for this rescue! The next winter, the extra grain we salvaged saved our family from starvation!

Chapter 18
My Sickness

Mother knit a fishing net from some flax twine. It was about 50' x 6' wide. In the middle it had an opening, ending in a narrowing point. The other boys and I looked forward to next summer's fishing possibilities. Later in August, we had some time available to go fishing. Because of the longer nights, the water was not as warm as we had wished. We remained in the water all day, only with a short lunch break. All we had to show was a medium sized carp.

That evening I experienced pain in my back. Even visiting the bone specialist did not provide any relief. Progressively the pain increased until I had to stay in bed. My knees and ankles swelled too. Walking caused great pain. To stay in bed was more comfortable. We tried all kinds of house remedies but with no relief.

Having time on my hands, I often read my Bible. Grandma occasionally came and talked to me for awhile. One night I dreamed of having a family of four children. Next morning I related this dream to Grandma. Though she said I was too young to think about these things, I still did. Could it be that I would get well?

Ice skating was our favorite sport in winter. One sunny afternoon following Christmas, my brothers went to the lake. As miserable as I felt, I bundled up, found the skates, and hobbled to the lake. My brothers helped me put on the skates. The exercise caused me to sweat and I noticed new movement returning to my joints. Excited, I came home and talked about it. From then on until spring, getting daily exercise was a priority.

The outdoors started to bloom with all kinds of flowers. Cherries were the first trees to come to life. Blossoms turned into berries and ripened in just a few weeks.

Strolling one midmorning through the fruit orchard, I saw a cherry tree loaded with dark ripe fruit. I had a craving for cherries and wanted to taste some. Since I did not have a ladder I pulled myself up into the tree and sampled the fruit. The taste was out of this world! I was totally full from eating the fruit. Not having any room to eat more, I let myself down to the ground. With amazement I looked at the ground which was strewn with cherry pits. I was amazed at how many cherries I had actually eaten!

As I walked home, the feeling of well-being in my joints increased by the second. My legs limbered up and the pain subsided considerably.

Arriving at home, I found the family sitting around the lunch table. I explained that I had eaten so many cherries I could not eat any more and that physically I felt markedly better. Mother asked why I did not bring any home. How could I without any container? After lunch I went and picked some for Mother. My health steadily improved and I was able to participate in the summer work schedule.

Chapter 19
New Help

Mother had been thinking about her sister and her husband who had died in Siberia. Although some of their children were grown up, Mother decided to invite them to come and live with us. They lost no time packing and came to live with us in southern Russia. They had five girls and one boy, Bill, a few years older than I. Now mother had the household help she needed. Bill helped us outside with whatever needed to be done.

Exploring The Estate

Youthful observations were impressed on my mind. Why were there so many wagons accumulated on grandfather's estate? How did they get here? Snooping and exploring around I noticed the building that housed the blacksmith shop with two furnaces, bellows, anvils, a bench with two vises, a large hand driven power drill and complete shop tools. What a treasure!

The adjacent room had carpenter benches with the appropriate equipment and tools. The third room housed some needed supplies. The evidence furnished the needed answer: grandfather's estate had built all the wagons from scratch.

Assembling the wheel impressed me most. The elements consisted of the wooden hub with the metal sleeve to fit the metal axle, flawless spokes, and a wooden rim made out of several parts, a metal rim, 1/4" x 2", cut about 1/2" shorter in circumference and welded, held it all together. I wondered, how this smaller rim would fit? A law of physics: when heated metal expands, when cooled quickly it contracts. I was amazed how much I learned by observation.

Various machinery would break down. There was no one we could turn to. I tried with my little knowledge, through observation, to repair things. By trying I succeeded. The big blacksmith shop and the carpenter benches were at my disposal. Tim left and married a girl who had worked for us and now was on his own.

Chapter 20

Education

The government now firmly in control, started to push for collectivization. New and strange laws were issued almost every week. Some of the old laws were repealed and religious freedom among the Russian populace began to spread. Many experienced a hunger for the Word of God and accepted the Gospel in simple faith.

Getting an education for all the children on the estate caused the parents to be concerned. As soon as we had moved from the business complex, Uncle John and parents hired private tutors. We now had an accelerated and far superior training than in the public school. It continued only intermittently after the typhoid epidemic was over.

During the lean years, city people started to arrive in our area. They brought all kinds of goods to trade for flour. Expensive jewelry and musical instruments were traded. My Uncles had obtained pianos for a sack of flour. Mother also got a piano and now wanted me to master the piano. For just room and board, a professor of music lived at one of my uncle's house. Not only did he teach uncle's children, but mother hired him and I had weekly lessons.

This continued weekly for nine months. Because of his age and the monotony of my practicing, the professor would drowse. As soon as he heard a mistake I had made, he slapped me on my hand gently. One day I had enough of it and would not come in for practice. Mother asked for the reason. I explained and the lessons were suspended.

Chapter 21
Step Dad

My father's oldest brother, John J's. wife, Emma, was a registered nurse and midwife. All of the young offspring claimed her as the one who brought us into the world. The stork story did not count with us. Uncle John J. and Auntie Emma had five children, two girls and three boys. Martin, their third son, died in 1919, and Aunt Emma followed him the following year.

In 1924 John J. married my mother. Our Step Dad planned for us children to live in his house. Some remodeling had to be done. As my brother and I were preparing the necessary materials, we were seized

Mother and Step Dad

with discouragement about living in a changed environment. We confronted Mother and rebelled against this idea. Mother and Step Dad than compromised. Instead of us moving in to his big house, he came to stay with us, and his children kept on living in his big house.

We noticed the immediate change in our household. A

Mother 's and Step Dad's families.

mature head was in control. At breakfast time Grandma usually read the Scripture and prayed. Now the head of the house assumed these duties. There was a lively conversation carried on at mealtime. Questions and answers were educational. We learned quite a lot.

Step Dad wanted the combined family photographed. The company's camera was produced and loaded with fresh film. I was asked to set up and focus it. Dad showed me how to develop the negatives and print the photographs. I was now the official photographer.

The Sunday gatherings were held at our house. Different members took part, but mostly Step Dad was in charge. Cousin John, Step Dad's oldest son, organized a choir. All of the youth participated.

Local choir - mostly cousins

Collectivization had top priority in the Soviet government. Dad lost no time in forming an official collective with all of us involved.His four children and all of us in the family were named. Now in official standing we had some priorities in obtaining modern machinery.

An American tractor, a Fordson, was purchased and I qualified to operate it. First training was necessary and for this provision was made to attend a two week seminar before delivery could be made. All the above was accomplished in the winter.

When springtime arrived, preparing the soil and the plowing was done with greater efficiency than with animals.

Surveyors to subdivide the land had come. A room was provided for them to stay with us. By order of the higher government authorities, some choice area was designated for a subdivision. The surveyors were out there, measuring six days a week. Sometimes they required assistance to hold the tape or drive a stake.

The younger surveyor brought some books over to my room on how to become active in the communist youth movement. Those books at the beginning derided religion and denied God completely. Just thinking on about what I read made me miserable.

Chapter 22

Spiritual Encouragement

At this time somehow a German printed magazine from Germany had arrived, With great interest I browsed through, stopping at a small article. The heading read: King Tut's Tomb Discovered. With great interest I continued reading about some wheat in the tomb was discovered. Grain that lay dormant over four thousand years had sprouted and grew like any other seed freshly sown. With amazement I was thinking surely the Bible can not be wrong. The God of creation created life, that spurns all infidels. With renewed confidence I continued reading my bible.

Some mysterious developments were evolving and we had no conclusive evidence as to their final ending.

Late in 1927 we were ordered to return the tractor. There was a heavy imposition of taxes which we scarcely could pay. Next Step Dad was summoned to appear before the district judge, to receive the notice that his voting privileges were cancelled. No longer was he a citizen.

Chapter 23
Planning to Leave the Soviet Union

For the previous five years, I diligently tried to obtain an exit visa to acquire higher education in America. Every year I had to furnish new evidence and additional passport money. The results were all the same: "Not this year." After I reached my twenty-first birthday, the answer now came strong and clear: "You serve the army first; then come back."

Writing to Odessa, a school of technology, had negative results: "We do not accept kulacks". Next I enrolled in a correspondence program and paid for two subjects: book keeping and writing in esperanto (universal) language.

In the fall of 1928, Brother Henry was sent to a school about fifty miles south by train. Step Dad explained to me that the family could spare Henry but not me. There was no one else to take care of the family.

The relationship with the younger brothers was based on the resistance to my orders. Both Henry and Willy worked well together. In later years Henry had to accept my partnership. On one of these assignments we were hauling hay into the barn.

Handing it up to me with the fork, he suddenly stopped, let the fork go, and jumped up and down several times. Staring ahead with a scared look, he suddenly grabbed his upper pants with both hands and squeezed. Relaxing he said: "I have got it!"

Quickly pulling off his pants, a dead field mouse was extricated. Before we went on the next trip, he found some binder twine and tied the the pants at the ankles. He said he did not want to be

Our family - a few days before I left.

scared anymore.

Sister Katja grew up to be a stout girl. She favored Mother when Mother was young. As as I was coming out of Grandma's room one day and Katja was coming out of the kitchen, we collided. Surprised I asked her if she was blind. She could not see me. Leading her to the light, she acknowledged that her left eye had no vision at all. I assumed that she was born that way. Only after meeting sister sixty-one years later, remembering about this incident, the following explanation was given:

Mother confessed one day that as an infant she had eye inflammation. With no physicians or drugstores close by, a home remedy was applied. As it came in contact with the eye, the child reacted violently. It was Mother's ignorance that caused sister lose the eyesight.

John was the oldest son of the Peters family. My playmates, Jacob and David, were next. Gerhard and a sister Anna besides an infant sister, were all the children they had as I recollect. Because of age differences, my association with John was casual.

In 1921 John disappeared and was not visible for some time. His family would not talk about him or his whereabouts. This year the typhoid epidemic had taken a large toll of relatives and friends. I thought John might have been one of the victims somewhere in a distant city where he had studied.

As quietly as he disappeared he showed up. Not having any knowledge where he had been, I met him outside. After greetings, our conversation centered around difficulties I encountered with the government and its reluctance in issuing exit passports. Casually I hinted that if a travel companion could be found to travel to the borders and cross unnoticed, I would risk it. John advised against it. I asked him his reason.

John now came out and unsolicitedly related his past year's experiences. He had crossed the Polish borders where they arrested and jailed him. Starvation and typhoid fever nearly finished him and he now was glad to return. "Not a second try for me, I've had enough of all the hardships," he said.

This tragic experience motivated me to try again and again. Every year an effort was made to obtain a visa until my twenty first birthday. An application to the school of technology in Odessa, was denied. Trying other educational institutions with the same results, the reason capitalist kulack.(oppressor)

Uncle Kroeker, father's second oldest sister's family sold their property, obtained visas and emigrated to Canada in 1926. Others were obtaining passports, why not I? I so desperately desired to leave before the draft call.

On September 6th. 1928 I turned age 21. Shortly after this a notice of induction arrived to report to the induction center on March 1st, 1929. Mother had watched all these years quietly for the hushed eventful news which was the discussion at the dinner table.

Distant relatives that were good friends of my parents came to stay at our house shortly after the new year of 1929. They were both experts in music and were teaching how to be a choir director. At dinner time, the visiting friends were discussing it with my parents, in a hushed voice. The words I clearly understood were "China" and "Henry." After everyone was dismissed, I approached Mother and asked for clarification of the subject.

Excitedly Mother told that Mr. Lowen's son, Henry, together with some Friesen sons in Siberia had successfully crossed into China. Knowing that I desired to get out of Russia, she asked if I had an opportunity, would I venture to go that route? I told her I surely would. That week Mother scraped up a small sum of money. No one knew about this anticipated venture beside Mother, me and Step Dad. Hastily a sleeping bag, a suitcase, and a wooden lunch box were prepared and packed. The time table for the train schedule was obtained, and departure planned for two A.M. February 2, 1929. The last evening Step Dad and I talked about money. All these years I had never asked for any, but now I needed some desperately. That week we had sold some livestock and he parted with eighty four rubles. We talked about leaving as a family now. He thought it could not get any worse. Besides his father died here and was buried and he also desired to be buried next to his father.

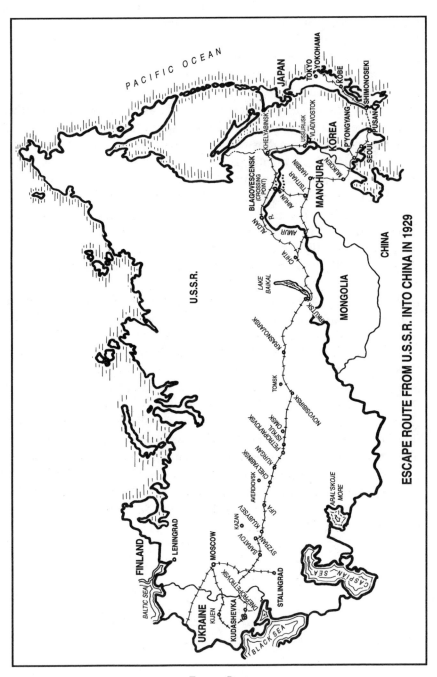

Escape Route

Chapter 24
Farewell Home

Shortly after midnight, Grandma, sister Katja,and brother Willy were summoned to the living room. I bade each one farewell and explained that I was leaving for a long trip. Since we dared not arouse any more disturbance, Willy helped me carry the luggage to the station. I did not mind being lightly dressed in this subzero weather. The load and the excitement kept me warm. One more thing I did: I surprised Willy, by kissing him goodbye and thanking him for the help.

When purchasing my ticket up to Icilkul, Siberia, the ticket agent said; "So you want to move to Siberia. Write when you get there, I also would like to move there."

Adding nothing to it, I left him with his conclusion.

The station was deserted and no one else knew about my presence there. Heavy thoughts and prayers occupied my mind for success. In December I had received army summons to report March first to the precinct. The distance to the China border had to be made in thirty days. The train arrived on schedule and I boarded my car.

At the next transfer station Dnepropetrovsk, while waiting, I bought a travel atlas. The next stations we passed were: Charkov, Voronez, Saratov and Kubychev, near the Volga, which at this time of the year was covered with ice and snow. Then came Ufa, Chelabinsk, Kurgan, Petropavlovsk and the destination Icil'cul. We passed the Ural mountains at night, so I did not see any of it.

Chapter 25
The Stopover In Siberia

The Thielmanns lived in a nearby settlement named Puchkovo. Relating my quest for a traveling companion, they suggested that one of their sons was in Moscow to obtain an exit visa. He might be back any time. It might profit for me to wait.

While waiting, the younger sons suggested a hunting party. Grouse was the only game bird available. I had a chance and fired without a hit. On the way home the story of wolf hunting was explained. The preparation required a fast running horse and a low light sleigh to hold three occupants. A young piglet was put in a sack and a dangling burlap sack on a long rope was tied to the sleigh. One driver and two men with loaded guns, one on each side, drove casually while at the same time tickling the little pig to make it squeal.

Wolves hearing this sound, would come running to investigate. Finding nothing in the sack, the wolf pack would then concentrate on the horse. The horse now was running at full speed. As the pack closed in, the sharpshooters waited for the ideal moment to pull the trigger. One after the other the wolves are eliminated. The rest of the pack quickly dispersed.

When we got back from the hunting of grouse, a telegram had arrived from Henry which read: "Am on my way to Blagovescensk, wire money."

It was evident that the Moscow trip was a failure. Picking up the address where I might locate Henry in that city, I departed.

Chapter 26

On the Train Again

Novosibirsk was another station, where I had to wait from morning till 8:00 P.M.. The unbearable cold pressed me to look around for some felt boots. Pricing them I decided to save the money and rather suffer. Later I discovered that being lightly dressed saved me from many embarrassing situations.

Some military personnel were traveling in the next train I boarded. As I watched them playing chess, they looked in my direction and asked if I would join them. At home when having company, chess had been our favorite game. One moved aside and I took his place. While setting up the pawns, I became apprehensive about what to answer if questioned. Silent prayer was my only solution.

Boldly they executed their moves, but I won the game. They now lost their interest in further playing. My behavior and attire impressed them that they had played with a young communist that knew his business. Those were the comments to each other.

The train was approaching the largest and deepest inland freshwater lake in the world, Lake Bajkal. A continuous flow of water emptied into the river Ankara. Someone on the train had mentioned that there were vendor stands at the station at Ankara that sold freshly caught fried fish. I was interested.

To get around the lake by train, we were passing through eighteen tunnels, a stretch of two hundred and and fifty miles, to link up with the rails going east from the lake. Being questioned, an elderly, knowledgeable person told the following story:

In 1905 Russia was at war with Japan. Fierce battles had drained war supplies. The only supplies available had to come by a track that was under construction and linked at the lake. Since, in this subzero weather, the ice measured fifteen feet thick, the engineers calculated it could hold up the weight of the train. Hastily rails were laid across the ice, and without a trial run, a loaded train ventured across full speed ahead. It did not make it! Supplies and men plunged to the depth of fifteen hundred feet.

With conventional methods, pick and shovel and the help of some dynamite, boring through eighteen tunnels, the rails were linked almost a year later. Russia lost the war for lack of supplies.

The train stopped at Ankara and I had enough time to get a fried fish and hot water for tea. What a treat they were instead of ham and bread for breakfast, noon, and supper.

Chita was the next stopover. We were informed that the train would go through on the RussoChina railroad, but our car would be coupled to another train that followed an alternate route, along the borders to our destination. Our car was maneuvered to the third rail; the train remained on the first.

While waiting and looking through the window, I read large letters written on the wall of a building opposite our car: "Money Exchange, Dollars Bought." It was also repeated in the Russian script.

I made a very thoughtless and dangerous move when I walked inside and asked if they sold dollars. The attendant looked surprised at me and said, "We only buy dollars." He briskly hurried into another room. It suddenly dawned on me that they would want to look at my I.D. and it must not happen at this point.

Realizing my error I quickly disappeared and stepped into the nearest car, out the other side, and into our car on the other track. I was greatly relieved after our car was coupled and the train moved out in the early P.M.

Another eight hundred miles to go. The Blagowescensk arrival was projected for early next morning where I wanted to get off. Almost at every stop I was awake. Passing the Aldan gold field station, some oriental passengers boarded. Noticing a vacant seat on the left side of the aisle, I moved and reclined in a sitting posture. Overcome with fatigue, I must have dozed off.

Chapter 27
The Escape

In a few hours my travel on the trans Siberian railroad would come to an end. From this single place my observation in both directions of the aisle was unobstructed. The uncertainty of the future and the behavior and next step to make laboriously weighed on my mind. I must have dozed. A hushed conversation and a flashlight pointed at certain passengers woke me up.

Without moving, I watched as these investigators were feeling the quilted clothes and then in different places cut them with razor blades. Also they were looking at their personal I.D. papers. It dawned on me that these men were searching for gold. These new passengers being searched had boarded the train at the Aldan station. The searchers must be K.G.B. men. At this point I was wide awake. With eyes closed I prayed and committed this situation into God's omniscient hands.

Inspecting every passenger, slowly they moved in my direction, pointing the light into my face, and then went on. What a relief! Praise and thanks for protection!

At the dawn of the day, we arrived at Blagovescensc.It was pretty nippy. The cloudless sky promised sunshine and with it warmer temperature. Walking through the station with all my baggage in hand, I looked around for some signs of an inn. One on the left had a large sign posted in front saying after three days you must register. I might stay here at least three days. Perhaps the party I was looking for could be located within this period of time.

I walked inside to the desk, paid the necessary fee and received a key for a padlock. The receptionist pointed in the direction of a room where individual beds were divided off and partitioned with plywood. Each room had a single bed,small table and no light; it was semi-dark. At least I could leave my things here. Next I consumed the balance of my ham and bread from the lunch box.

On March first I was some six thousand miles away from my induction precinct! All sorts of dramas ran through my mind. What if I were apprehended. Twenty-one years of age, having risked everything, what would be next? I needed council and courage to replace fear. Meditating and praying for help in my next steps, I praised and thanked the Lord for helping me to this point.

Stepping outside into the heavy snow and the quiet under a bright cloudless sky, I found sunshine facing me. The direction pointed east. Someone already had made a path through the snow. Now it was easy to follow. I noticed the high ground that the walkway was on and how it slanted down to the river that was frozen solid. Not quite a mile across lay the Chinese city Sachalian. From here it looked simple. What about the border guard?

After locating the street number of the Baptist church, I walked inside. The pastor, getting ready for next day's worship service, stood in the hall. He introduced himself. After I had asked for my kinsman, Henry Thielmann, he became apologetic as he did not know his mission. I confessed my relationship to Henry and told him it was of utmost importance for me to locate him. He obliged, looked up the address where Henry stayed, and handed it to me.

Chapter 28
Locating New Friends

Arriving at the given address, I knocked at the door and asked for Henry Thielmann. The lady went inside. Henry came to the door and I introduced myself. Being invited inside, I was introduced to his friends: Aaron and Agatha Langemann, George and Maria Froese, and their mother, Mrs. Balzer. The latter also was the stepmother of Agatha. None had children. Altogether there were six and I was the seventh in the party. After their initial shock had dissipated, they wanted to know more about me.

Openly and without hesitation I unfolded my whole story. For the past five years I had unsuccessfully tried to obtain a visa.In1928 the final answer given me was to serve my tour in the army; then they might consider a visa. March first was my reporting date and I am six thousand miles away. And within three days I has to be out of there.

This new thought gave them an impetus to finalize their own plans. The preparations they had to make took more than three days. Since they were renting, Aaron asked the landlady if she would allow one more house guest for a few days. She agreed to it. Then I was requested to stay the limited time at the inn, and then move in with them.

Chapter 29

Preparation

Plans jelled quickly because of me and because of the early ice melting possibility that might make the river unsafe to cross. Aaron explained that they planned on buying two horses with harness and two sleighs, drive several miles out of the city, and then cross the ice into China. The questions then asked were if I agreed to the plan, and if I would share in the expenses. I agreed.

The ladies had prepared a hearty lunch and invited me to share. I had missed this for so long. Before dark I went back to my cubicle at the inn.

After a restful night, I felt better. In the morning I had to get some bread for breakfast. It was not difficult to spot a bakery. Walking outside, I noticed a human line. Walking over I saw a sign that said "Bakery" and I joined the line. The line moved slowly and shortly before I reached the door, they announced, "We are out of bread. Next batch will be ready in one hour."

Some people left but I could not abandon my place in the line. After more than an hour, I got my pound of bread.

The third day I moved in with the group. Next day we all went to church. Pastor Wiens preached a heartwarming message.A group of young communists had infiltrated and were causing a disturbance. The pastor admonished them sternly and suggested for them to leave if it did not please their ears.

Monday was farmer's market. The men decided to go and make the agreed purchases. I dared not to show myself in an open place. I stayed put at home. Not only did they buy the horses but took them to the blacksmith shop and had them shooed on all four hooves. The delightful long awaited moment came nearer, when expectations might turn into reality.

One more detail the men were looking for a farmer to travel ahead of us about five or six hundred yards so we could be signaled if any troops or border patrol came in sight. They found a Dutch farmer at the market and invited him to the house.

The next day the farmer arrived, Aaron explained to him our desire was that he be our signal man. He vehemently refused to make this kind of a deal. On Aaron's part it took a considerable amount of explaining. He would in no way jeopardize his act. Besides we were going to pay him. Would he take thirty five rubles? He hesitated. "We'll give you forty." That clinched the agreement.

Signals and identification had to be worked out in detail. At eight a.m. we would have the two sleighs and horses loaded with a bale of hay, feed for the animals, and a bucket tied in the rear of the first load.

The farmer would have a horse-drawn-wagon and his family with him for identification. For further recognition it was prearranged that he would use the whip on the horse and say, "Get going." No words were to be exchanged. We would follow him at a distance of about seven hundred yards. If he came around a bend of the river that was hidden from our view and it was clear of border guards, the farmer was to step off on the right side of his buggy; the opposite, if the guards were present. We were able to see what was behind us.

Chapter 30

The Crossing: March 8th, 1929

Early next morning, after breakfast, we committed our affairs and lives to the Keeper of our souls. The day before the ladies laundered everyone's underwear. The seating was arranged; Aaron and Agatha with Henry would be in the first sleigh. George, Maria, Mrs. Balzer and I would be in the second one.

We had stationed ourselves at the outskirts of the city and were waiting. A long transport of horse drawn sleighs, over sixty loaded with grain and accompanied with cavalry soldiers, were approaching the city from the east. We just had to wait.

After one hour, our guide showed up. The road now was clear and we lagged behind as prearranged. It was a warm day. The zero weather was welcome.

We traveled possibly two hours, when the signal man stepped off to the river side. The rear was clear of any traffic. Aaron in the first sleigh veered to the right and was on the ice. George, who was driving the second sleigh, did the same. My heart started to pound rapidly. Seated in the rear, I fell off when the sleigh hit the ice. Getting up and running to catch up shocked me to my senses.

This fast flowing river was a large body of water from the Himalaya mountains and had some ice floes frozen in an upright position. Under the snow the floes are not visible. Our sleigh landed on one and got stuck. The horse promptly got out of harness and stopped. Noticing our predicament, Aaron halted his horse and came running to help us to put the animal back to work. As we were approaching the land, we noticed some men waving us to go back. They must have been wood choppers. Since they were quite a distance to the left, we proceeded and reached the top. Now we could see that this was only an island! We had to cross another part of the river. Proceeding south down the bank, the horses plunged into the snowdrift and would not move. All three men went and made a path through the snow, and pulled the first horse and sleigh through. The second would follow on his own. We reached the other side without any further obstruction.

It was exactly twelve o'clock noon when we reached the Chinese border. We let the horses rest, and congratulated each other for having made this crossing. Next we bowed and praised the Lord for His protection.

Chapter 31
China

No one had taken time to take liquid or lunch along. The excitement was so great. By the grace of God we had made it. Totally unfamiliar, in a strange country, what next? Which way to turn? It took us three hours to get to this point. An equal amount of time would be used up to get to the Chinese city opposite Blagovescensk, where we came from. Having rested for about twenty minutes, we turned west.

Since we could not see any road, tracks, or houses, we moved up to higher ground and followed our instincts west. The animals were exhausted.To lighten the load some of us walked. It was close to sunset when we reached the suburban area of Sahaljan.

With our spirits still high, walking now on the city street, we encountered a Chinese border patrol of about twelve men. The leader stopped us and asked in the Russian language where we had come from and demanded visas. Our explanation did not satisfy him. Part of his detachment he sent on and we were taken to head quarters for interrogation.

After a thorough search and request for visas allowing us to stay in China, we were locked up in the local jail. The animals were taken where they could be fed. We also each received a bowl of thin gruel of grits. They allowed us our bedding and we laid it out on a six foot deep bench, constructed along one wall. The temperature in the room was comfortable.

Reflection time now at hand, thoughts came to surface. What vent wrong? The persecution complex welled up in me. What if they return us? The others might get possibly five years imprisonment. I as a draft dodger would be executed. Physical and emotionally exhausted, I had a fitful night. Only God could help us.

In the morning first the men and then the women were taken out for relief. After the same thing for breakfast we had last night we started to talk about what to do next. Where from here. It seemed that no one had a solution. Aaron knocked a few times on the gate for an attendant for information that the attendant could not give.

All that day and half of the following morning I maintained

a silent prayer vigil, requesting for the Lord to intervene in our situation. Shortly before noon I experienced a euphoria and an assurance we would be released. Immediately I relayed to Mrs.Balzer that we would be released. She asked me how I knew. I explained to her the Lord just now had given me the assurance.

A local Japanese innkeeper, with a Russian wife, who also spoke the Russian language, hearing of our incarceration, came to the prison with a loaf of bread. Talking to him, Aaron inquired what he could do to get us out of this predicament.On the third day towards evening we were released into the custody of the innkeeper. What a relief! We gave Thanksgiving to God for His gracious assistance in these most crucial and difficult moments in life.

What are values? In this instance,liberty outshines all others! It felt good to shake off all suspicion of being followed. We now are at liberty to believe and express ourselves freely. Praise the Lord!

Moving into the inn of our benefactor, sleeping places were assigned to each and we were advised that dinner was ready.

All seven of us, with grateful hearts and minds, gave hearty thanks for deliverance and now for this bountiful banquet. The menu consisted of a small broiled bird; it must have been a quail. The vegetables were potatoes, cabbage, bread and we had tea. To me this fantastic meal tasted incredible beyond description. Never before or since have I eaten delicious food like this.

The following day the men sold the horses and the equipment. In the late afternoon an officer of the guard came over and demanded that we pay him for assisting us. He told us that the Soviet government had offered sixty dollars for each person he returned back. We paid him.

Our next destination was Harbin. The only transportation from Sahaljan to Tsitsihar, the next railroad connection, was by bus. We were informed the bus did not operate in the winter. It would be two more weeks before the ground would give traction to bus tires.

Other refugees arrived. A single young man, Henry Koslow, two years older than I, defected. A middle aged man from the Baptist church also joined us.

At the appointed day the bus pulled up in front of the hotel. We boarded it and off we went. A wagon trail acted as our highway. Two hundred and eighty miles had to be navigated in this fashion. At any incline in the road the men got off and helped to push the bus up. At this rate, we covered half the distance the first day.

In the morning, after staying over night in a village, we had difficulty getting the opium drugged driver to get going. By four o'clock we arrived at the station.

On the train to Harbin.

What a shock to see the Soviet and the Chinese flags waving in the breeze. It was explained that in this part of Manchuria, the railroad was a joint operation.

I utilized a two hour waiting period, to be alone for meditation. I had not wasted any money. The last was used for bus fare. There was none left for the train ticket.How to get from here to Harbin? No solution was in sight.

While sitting at this solitary table by myself for some time, Aaron and George walked up from behind. Laying his hand on my shoulder Aaron said, "John, we know that you are out of money. We'll help you until you can pay it back." Thank you Lord for solving this problem!

We boarded the train on schedule. My amazement had no end. How is it possible that Russian personnel operated this rail road system inside a capitalistic government. Later it was explained that at the borders, non-communist crews took over.

The pioneer of defecting from Soviet Russia into China by horse and sleigh, Mr. John Friesen, expected us at the Harbin station. Aaron must have notified him somehow. Being versatile and domesticated in Harbin, he informed Aaron about living quarters and how much rent to pay. With all greeting formalities dispensed, Aaron and George left to look for a house. Upon their return a horse drawn taxi hauled our belongings to the new address. Located in the suburban area, the house had three bedrooms and a kitchen. A wood stove heated the dwelling and also acted as a surface plate. Henry Koslow slept on the kitchen couch: I slept on the floor. The rest were comfortable in their individual bedrooms.

Friends that traveled together.

Chapter 32
Experiences in China

Orientation (getting acquainted) in this large city of Harbin with its influx of many refugees was our priority. I had listed work as number one. Henry K. and I teamed up and walked the streets from morning until evening. Since most of the department stores and other establishments had Russian speaking employees, it was relatively easy to get around and find information. Everywhere we asked the answer resulted the same: "We do not sign up any more job seekers." When the monarchist army, the White Russians, lost to the Red army, the Communist, several million people retreated into China. Harbin and vicinity absorbed the major bulk. All men were trained soldiers, but very few had any particularly useful skills. Hence some officers of high rank, served as door keepers. They wore their full uniform and army decorations while on the job.The prospect of finding employment looked pretty dim. A Scripture came to mind: "Ask and you shall receive, seek and you shall find, knock and it will be opened to you." With this in mind, I could not go wrong because Jesus said it.

Nights were the only suitable moments when I could quietly meditate, think and pray. The night weather in March still pointed out that Mr.Frost controlled the atmosphere. The cold temperature reflected its influence through my thin sleeping bag. The house could not be heated for lack of fire wood. Feeling miserable, I stayed awake most of the nights. I had to make body movements to keep feet and body warm.

I had not written my folks of the successful crossing and safe arrival at the destination. The content of the letter to be written, disturbed me. A voice inside of me suggested, "Haven't you been rebellious at times? Has it not hurt your folks?"

With remorse and repentance I confessed this wrong doing to the Lord and resolved to write in this letter an apology and a request for forgiveness. I wrote the letter. In the morning, I enclosed the return address and promptly mailed it.

A grocery store, located at the next corner of the street, had a large steam kettle outside with a whistle. When the water temperature reached the boiling point, it whistled to let customers know tea water was ready. The price of this tea water was only a few pennies. Henry K., Mrs. Balzer and I teamed up and had our meals as a trio. The others had their separate arrangements.

Looking for work and passing by the department store where one of the generals acted as doorkeeper, I was compelled to talk to him. After asking a few questions, my story unfolded to him in a few sentences. After he realized that I basically was a farmer and knowledgeable with machinery and tools, he said, "This company has a separate farm implement store. The general superintendent is visiting this store today and as soon as he comes out, I'll signal and you can tell him what you told me."

In a little while, the gentleman described appeared, when I explained my need, he suggested I meet him the next morning at nine. He gave me the address of the implement store.

Cooking outside.

Waiting, ahead of the given hour, I met the superintendent as he went into the office. He noticed and greeted me. It was quite a while before both gentlemen came out. He must have not spoken about me to the manager. My presence reminded him, and motioning me to approach said, "This young man has knowledge about farm implements, thought you might want to interview him."

In the office some more questions were answered. The manager promised to pay one dollar a day. And I was to show up the next morning. Outside he introduced me to the foreman. Elated I brought this good news home.

Being versatile I had a good rapport with the foreman and other employees. Crates with dull plow bottoms started to arrive. They needed to be sharpened. The foreman put me to work with the blacksmith. In about a week and a half, the other man quit and I continued until the end of April.

It was surprising how far a dollar stretched. In the morning for breakfast we had tea and bread. In the evening, we ate bread and tea. At noon I walked to the nearby restaurant. The menu consisted of soup and bread, vegetables and meat. For thirty-five cents I would buy half of the menu and periodically change off from soup and bread to vegetables and meat. Gratefully I accepted this survival diet.

By now two hundred fifty refugees of Mennonite origin had arrived. All wanted to migrate, if possible, to Canada or the U.S.A. Most were families. Since Mr. John Friesen arrived first, he was elected as leader of this group. Mr. Friesen had a friend in Dr. John Isaac, an eye specialist, who treated all families of the foreign attaches. Being on speaking terms with all of the ambassadors, Dr. Isaac discovered that Canada would not negotiate with this group, but the American ambassador would. Mr. Friesen then was requested to write a resume and specify why we had left Russia.

This article was translated into English and forwarded to President Hoover. Being in charge of the relief agency during the postwar period of 1920, President Hoover knew the history of these refugees.

When this request was presented to the Congress, they voted to allow these two hundred fifty refugees to be processed for entrance into the U.S.A. beginning in August of 1929 in groups of 15-20 every month.

Chapter 33
Life in Harbin

We started to visit the Russian Baptist church as soon as we got there, for worship and fellowship. There were many things different from the churches in the Soviet Union. The members all were well dressed and well fed. No fear could be noticed in anyone's behavior. A loving likable spirit prevailed.

Late in April, as soon as the snow had all melted, activities picked up in the purchase of farm implements. In this vast land of Manchuria, parcels of land were doled out for those who promised to cultivate it. Wealthy generals took advantage of it and bought tractors and appropriate farm implements. The opportunity for me had come to go as a tractor operator. The promise was $80.00 a month, an override bonus on every plowed acre, and room and board free. I accepted this offer. The departure was scheduled for late the same evening.

At home we all had a profitable discussion about the departure possibility to America, I requested them to be sure to keep me informed. I asked Henry K. if I found there were possibilities to hire more help, if he would accept a position. He agreed.

Henry Thielmann had found a way to go to Germany and left earlier. America had no attraction for him.

Russian Baptist church in Harbin

Gathering all my belongings including a box camera with an adequate supply of films, I left for the station.

Chapter 34
On the Field of Manchuria

The place in question where I was supposed to work was half way from Tsitsicar and the Russian border. The supervisor for my new employer met me at the station. A horse with a two wheeled cart had the fuel supplies and provision loaded. The driver, our cook, and the supervisor on top led the way.I followed with the tractor and plow.

About 12 miles to the east was a small walled village with a few mud houses where the supervisor lived. We drove on two miles farther and set up a tent. A dugout already existed for the cook and kitchen. The supervisor and the cook both understood the Russian language.

The helper arrived the next day. He was twice my age, married, and a former low ranking officer in the former czarist army. He was Polish by race and had a family. He knew how to drive a truck, but had no knowledge of agriculture.

The neighbors to our parcel, six men with two tractors of International Harvester make, were also living in tents. All were soldiers with no farm experience. Because they were swamped with work, we were requested to help them out in this spring season. The fall plowing needed to be harrowed and made ready for planting. Both tractors worked eight hours per day each for two weeks.

Work did not progress fast enough. The supervisor asked if I could find a third driver. A letter went off to Henry K. offering him fifty dollars per month. I would teach him how to handle the

Rural Transportation.

tractor. In a few days he showed up. Now work went on around the clock.

Working at this pace for almost a month, the emergency was over and the third man was not needed. I had to decide who was to be dismissed, Henry or the family man. My vote was against the soldier and he left. It was a difficult but a wise decision. For my standard of morals, I needed a like minded companion in this part of the world.

Plowing.

Housing and supplies.

We plowed every day except on Sundays. Close to the middle of June the supervisor had scheduled us to move closer to the Russian border. This is as close as I wanted to be. Tractor and equipment were all readied But border clashes occurred between the Russians and the Chinese armies. Heavy troop movements were conducted on the railroad we were supposed to travel on. We had to wait it out. I questioned the supervisor if he would want to dismiss us and he replied that the boss wanted to keep us.

The supervisor found it unsafe for us to live in the tent outside the wall and requested that we move inside. Here we cleaned the tractor motor and took it apart. While the pistons were exposed, a crowd of onlookers had gathered. Heatedly they debated in a language we did not understand. I asked the supervisor what they were arguing about. He interpreted that the old men think that there are devils inside that make the engine work. I explained that the fuel explodes inside and pushes against the pistons, which in turn operate the wheels. He translated into Chinese.

A letter from Step Dad had come, a reply to my request.

They had forgiven me long before I requested. Also they said that the K.G.B. was looking for me until he informed them that he received a letter that I was in China. They quit snooping.

Writing another letter, as agreed, I advised them to go west. They knew what I meant. The escape route east was not advisable.

Eating lunch.

Inside view of walled in houses.

Chapter 35

The Culture In China

The Chinese government at that time had stabilized. The feuding and warring lords, with their small armies, were in a subdued spirit. People were looking for work here in the north from as far south as Fuzhou and Canton. Men would leave their families and venture to find earning possibilities in this new developing area. Earned wages were sent home to sustain their loved ones. Some had not seen their families for years. Men with better earnings let them come as soon as feasible.

The row crop farming was done by horse drawn scrappers and hand hoeing. The seed was dropped into the furrow and covered. When the plants had grown, the weeds were removed with

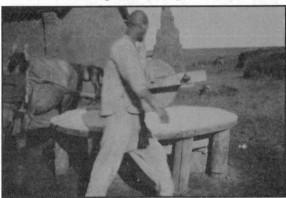
Domestic flour mill.

the hoe. All harvesting was done by scythe or sickle. A horse drawn, grooved, round stone was pulled over spread sheaves on flat ground for the threshing. An elevated platform with a huge stone wheel and an axle through the middle of it acted as the flour mill. A blindfolded horse was hitched to the stone and a man walked with a whisk broom, sweeping the uncrushed grain under the wheel until everything was finely ground.

Pork and chicken were the main meat contributors of food. Beef was expensive. Occasionally hunters succeeded in trapping some of the wild red antelopes which roamed the semiflats of Manchuria by the thousands. The antelopes were the size of a goat. Both male and female had round curved horns to the back. This very swift animal grazed in large herds and never separated.

The natives had a unique way of hunting these antelopes without the use of a gun. A hole was dug in the ground about 3' x 8' x 7' deep in the area where the grass was tall. The hole was carefully camouflaged with thin brush and grass.About five to seven horseback riders were used. After they encircled the herd, the whole mass was funneled into the desired area. With increased tempo and ever closer formation, the animals ran for their lives. A few would fall in the hole.Once the opening was exposed, the rest jumped over it. Usually several of these animals were trapped. These traps were scattered all over the land. Some were visible; others, where high grass existed, remained hidden.

Our supervisor decided it was more profitable to work than loaf. Off we went to the area where we had worked before. Past the last parcel we measured a very large section of land. The length was probably a mile. We stationed Henry on the south end with a tall flag on a pole. I with the tractor went north to the point of beginning. In order to make a straight furrow, my eyes were riveted on the flag and the radiator cap. Not paying any attention to my surroundings in the low land the tractor fell into one of those hidden traps. I reversed the gear, but the machine would not respond. The whole contraption was embedded to deep. The front wheels were inoperable because of the damaged steering system.

A tractor from the other camp was summoned to pull our tractor out. The supervisor got angry with me. Why had I not looked? I responded that's exactly what I had done. My eyes were focused on the goal. Besides,the hole was obscured. A new part was ordered and in a few days we had the tractor going again.

In this vast isolated area, social life did not exist. Sundays were granted as a rest day. Henry and I,being like minded, did not participate in the wild orgies and drunkenness of the other camp. It would not have been noticeable unless the supervisor had not brought it up.

Questioning me he asked, "John, what motivates you to live the way you live? You don't drink or have prostitutes come to your camp. What do you believe?"

This challenge I had not expected. Answering him I said, "The Bible tells me that God created the whole world and mankind and that I am to live to honor Him with my life."

Adding he said, "I have no desires in this world. I smoke three dollars worth of opium a month but would like to smoke as much as my boss." I asked how much? He said, "Three dollars a day." Because of the abundance of dust, we had a breakdown of the magneto on the tractors electrical system. Someone had to take the part into Harbin. My request to go was granted. With some instructions to his boss, the supervisor gave me the needed fare money and I left that evening.

Arriving before sunrise, I walked to the residence where friends lived. Surprised that I got there this early, unannounced, they invited me for breakfast. As soon as the implement office was open, the magneto was exchanged. Then a long walk led me to the superior's residence, delivering the information he desired.

Until the train departure at four p.m.,I visited with friends. Aaron informed me that Mr.Friesen and James Isaac, Dr.Isaac's younger brother, had departed for America to find passage assistance for those that lacked it.

An hour after arrival on the field next morning, we were in business plowing.

Our cook by the name of Lee, probably past fifty, had an accommodating personality. In his limited knowledge of the Russian language, he asked us what kind of menu we preferred. We suggested soup and occasional meat with vegetables. In meats only pork and mutton were available. We preferred mutton.

The first over-seasoned soup he made we could not swallow. But from then on he improved. We were well fed and had no

Our cook, Lee.

complaints about food. His habit of drinking hanchy [rice brandy] before and after meals and before going to bed amazed me. How could he sustain this habit? Sometime later I discovered that he traded our benzene for the hanchy.

The tractor engine needed benzene for starter fuel. When warmed up, we switched over to regular slow burning coal oil or kerosene supplied by the Shell Oil Company. The fuel came in five gallon cans. A hole was punched in one corner with a smaller in the other for air and than dumped into the engine tank. A five gallon benzene supply would last us for a considerable time.

In a hurry one after noon after I had opened a new can of benzene, I plugged it up with a wooden cork. After walking a distance, Lee came out with a bottle in his hand, knelt down and filled his container with benzene, and disappeared in the dugout. I immediately returned, soldered up the hole with tin, and went about my business. Every time we used benzene, the hole was soldered.

Lee must have gotten low on his brandy. While closing up the hole, he confronted me and asked me why I was soldering up the can? I answered that benzene evaporates awfully fast. He now confessed that he needed hanchy and this was the only way he could afford it. I suggested that he talk it over with the supervisor.

While making the rounds on the tractor, a small miniature structure was silhouetted against the horizon. One free Sunday I walked over to inspect it. It looked like a small temple, hewn out of white, soft sandstone and beautifully decorated. It was about five feet tall. On the lower shelf were signs of burned incense sticks. I could not make any sense out of a structure that far from civilization.

Next time I had business with the supervisor, I asked about this structure. The tale went like this:

A wealthy merchant traveling this way, was being pursued by bandits. In his distress he vowed to his god that if he protected him and he got out of the distress, he would build him a temple there.Miraculously the merchant hid in the tall grasses and escaped his pursuers.

The incense was being burned there by local people.

It was a delight to behold the newly planted crop growing and now in need of being harvested. After assembling the

Miniature temple.

ordered binder, we were in business. Small crowds were watching as the sheaves, one after another, were expelled from the binder. It really amazed everyone, this first crop grown on this virgin soil.

Harvesting.

By the end of August, the temperature dropped at night by quite a few degrees. Henry decided that he would like to quit and return to the city. Receiving his pay, he departed.

The supervisor found a native young chap with mechanical inclinations, but no tractor knowledge. After a few days with him he was like an old pro.

Not having cold weather clothes, I also resigned about the middle of September. Reviewing my situation up to this point, I could not help but praise the Lord for providing free room and board, for good health and no expenses. I was able to earn $640.00. The supervisor had provided a one horse cart to take me and my few belongings to the railroad station.

The time spent there was profitable educationally. I learned firsthand to observe the domestic life of the Chinese culture. Children were being married at the early age of twelve and thirteen years. Their count of age begins at conception. The women had small feet and were walking as if on stilts.

Chinese Wedding

Chapter 36

New Horizons

Next morning I was in the company of friends again. I went shopping the first thing. It felt so much nicer to be dressed from head to foot as a gentleman again. What a difference instead of working all summer in shorts.

The exciting news was that we were put on the emigration list. Passage money was available for those who did not have it. Our departure time schedule coincided with Christmas. It was a time of rejoicing. Also I paid Aaron my debt, owing him forty dollars.

The landlady had a one room apartment, into which Henry and I

Back in the city.

moved. Attending church gatherings was greatly appreciated. Physical checkups and vaccinations were performed and passport issued. We received permission from Aaron to use the address of his aunt in Reedley, California, where he was going. I promptly forwarded it to my parents in Russia as my mailing address.

The Friesen family had an invalid son, Abe, with whom I got acquainted. At present it was not possible to obtain a visa for him. He would be left behind in China until arrangements could be made. I visited him periodically and whatever need he had, I took care of it.

Chapter 37

In Transit

The day of departure had come. On December twenty fourth, eight p.m., we boarded the train. It would take us all night and the next day to reach the tip of Korea.

It was a very unusual experience to have Christmas on a train. Some pleasant but some unpleasant experiences in Russia came into review. And what about the future? He who knows the end from the beginning, into His hands I was committed. Some time during the night our cars were switched in Mukden and diverted to go to Korea.

Stopping in Seoul some time in midmorning, I noticed some vendors selling festive items. Leaving the car for a closer inspection, I purchased some praised Korean sweets. Observing the culture of this people and the faces, there was only a slight difference in the costume and in the complexion. By late evening we had reached the tip of the peninsula. In the port city of Pusan we transferred to a ferry going to Japan.

While still dark in the morning, we left the rocking ferry and transferred in Shimonoseki to a train that would carry us to Yokohama. The train inspector who demanded our fare tickets, did at first not understand that our passage was included in our pass. It resolved itself after the language barrier was removed.

In Yokohama we walked to our lodging place. Entering the building, the lady pointed to our feet and said something in

On the ship to U.S.A.

Japanese. We got the point of taking off our shoes before entering a room. The climate was not as severe as Siberia, but still below freezing. Conventional European furniture was missing. The modest dinner was served on low tables and we ate while kneeling. We slept on the floor on mats. After breakfast we were carted off to the harbor and boarded the ship "Taio Maru."

For the next thirty days "Tio Maru" acted as our home. Being third class passengers, we were made comfortable on the lower deck in front of the ship on bunk beds. The freight loading lasted another day. Someone made the suggestion that we see the countryside. There were no takers.

The freight being put away, passengers boarded, the planks were pulled in, and everything made seaworthy. A loud whistle blasted and the tug boats pushed and pulled the vessel into self propelled position. The confetti started to tear and soon all the physical ties were severed.

We gained considerably in temperature as the ship headed southeast towards the Hawaiian Islands. After a few days in the open sea, a typhoon hit us and we were compelled to stay inside.

Not having any ill effects or sea sickness, I roamed the ship and inspected every area permitted. Somewhere I found an inscription written in the German language: Kaiser Wilhelm Schiff. Asking the ship personnel about it, they gave the

Friends on deck.

following explanation: In World War 1, the Allies requested help from Japan. Responding toward the end of hostilities, Japan got this ship and a few other items as consolation prize.

The ship's diet gave me no problem. Others, as soon as they came on deck, ran to the railing and fed the fish. Most were affected with sea sickness.

Geography was one of my favorite subjects in school and crossing the time zone for the first time excited me. We had two

Sundays also and also two days with the same date.

At Honolulu of the Hawaiian Islands, the ship had to unload some cargo and would be tied down all day. We were given permission to get off, but were told to be back by five p.m. The walking on solid ground did us good. Some passengers went shopping, others wanted to see the beaches, but most were interested in the acclaimed fruit.

Chapter 38
Arrival In San Francisco

San Francisco would be reached in six days. The ship docked outside the Golden Gate at five o'clock in the morning. Cargo inspectors and immigration personnel arrived. The passengers were assembled in the main lobby of the ship and were asked to produce their passports. When my turn came, the lady officer asked how much money I had. I told her I had fifteen dollars. She closed her book and said, "You cannot come in." What a shock! Confusing thoughts raced through my mind. An older travel companion approached me and I related the words of the officer. He assured me that everything would be as scheduled.He who trusts the Lord will never be put to shame. All the immigrants were taken to Angel Island for processing. Next morning after all physical and biological testing was done, a boat returned us to the ship we came on."Tio Maru" had docked at Pier #42. Waiting at the railing to be disembarked, a few hands on the dock waved at us. We recognized Mr.Friesen and a few others were introduced to us after we had stepped on the dock. Rev. Eitzen, the elder from the Mennonite church in Reedley,about 200 miles southeast, including a few other members from his community, came to take us to our destination. One more time we had to go to the immigration office, to pick up our "I.D." papers on which was stamped the day of our entry, January 30th, 1930. Interesting that we were able to communicate with these gentlemen in the German language.

Late in the afternoon, Henry, another single man and I were seated in the automobile belonging to Mr. John Enns. While driving,he encouraged us to help ourselves to some oranges he had along. To keep the driver awake, we communicated until late in the night. When we arrived at his place, beds were all made and before retiring, Mr. Enns informed us breakfast would be at seven o'clock in the morning.

I slept in. When I came down from the upstairs bedroom, everyone was sitting around the table waiting for me. After calmness was established, Mr. Enns read from the Bible a fitting portion for this occasion and prayed, thanking the Lord for grace and protection and for the food about to be participated in. The first typical American breakfast which I had ever eaten was cornflakes with milk (which I had not tasted before), bread and butter with cheese, and coffee.

Our permanent address must have been discussed prior to our arrival. Mr. Enns said he would take us now to the place where we would live. A few minutes from the farm and we were in town, where he parked in front of "M" street. We thanked Mr. Enns for his kindness in bringing us here. He then left to deliver the other young man to his parents.

Chapter 39

Life In America

Three single men introduced themselves, Henry and John Friesen, sons of Mr.Friesen, and Henry Loewen, the nephew. These three young men, were the first ones that ventured the crossing

House on M street, Reedly

of the Amure river into China in early winter of 1928. Henry Loewen wrote to his father, who conducted choir director training seminars in our area in the Ukraine. Through him I got the idea to go to China.

After the formalities we delved into the details of cohabitation. Henry F., being the oldest, explained to us how much each of us had to come up with in cash each month; five dollars which included the utilities. For groceries we had to add whatever the cost outlay was. Since their sister, Anna, did the housekeeping, she was included in this family free of expenses. We consented to everything.

To my surprise, Mrs. Wiens lived on Eleventh Street, just around the corner. Aaron with his wife, and George and his wife with their mother all lived in a small cottage in Mrs. Wiens' back yard. This lady was such a nice person, making inquiries as to the well-being of my parents. I asked if it was all right to have given her address to my parents to communicate with me. It created no problem. As soon as letters arrived, she would bring them over.

The employment situation looked dismal. No one worked in this farming community in the winter. The only crop to be coming in shortly was oranges. Pruning vineyards also might be a possibility if one knew how. On Monday night the local high school had evening classes in various skills including the english language. Learning the language appealed to all of us.

We arrived on Thursday and now the weekend had come.

The men were indoctrinating us as to the events and program of the church.

Sunday morning we all walked to church. The service began at 9:00 a.m. The entire group that had arrived, were present. After a few preliminaries, Rev. Eitzen made us stand up, extended an official welcome, and bade us feel at home in America.

The language of the service was conducted in German, and we were able to understand. Mr. Friesen participated by reading Psalm 137. He also made a few appropriate remarks about what the newly arrived had experienced in the land they fled from. He concluded with thanks for our safe arrival and petitioned the Lord for guidance in this new land. It was an impressive service long to be remembered.

The Mennonite Brethren Church in Reedley made a lasting influence on my spiritual life. Getting acquainted with various spiritual leaders enhanced my concept on different issues and life in America. In particular did I value and esteem Rev. Eitzen, Rev. Jacob Hofer, Rev. Huebert and Henry Martens, and many other unnamed citizens, whose help and advice I greatly appreciated.

Church on the right.

Chapter 40
Reedley

The house on "M" street had two bedrooms, one bath, a living room, kitchen, screened back porch and a small basement half in the ground, which made the building much taller than the rest of the houses on the street. The furniture consisted of four beds, five chairs, and a table in the kitchen where we also had our meals. The living room had a built in china closet with drawers on the bottom half. Henry F. told us boys we were going to sleep there. The mattresses were in the closets of the front bedroom. In the morning, we were to role them up and put them back again. These were the living accommodations. The backyard had a one-car garage with the entrance from the alley that served as shelter for the Friesen brother's 1929 two door Ford sedan.

The topic of depression was on everybody's mind, from the years of plenty of high prices on farm products and wages, to no market for farm products and high unemployment and no buyers. An epidemic of infantile paralysis hit this community without knowledge of its origin or cure. It seemed as if it were contagious.

Our quest for work continued day after day. Occasionally some of us would find some farm work, but the main promise of work was picking oranges in April. The weekly routine consisted of going to church on Sunday and attending all services. On Monday night after dinner all six of us piled into the Ford and off we went to night school. Mrs. McElroy, a short stout lady, had excellent teaching abilities to help the newcomers learn the pronunciation and spelling of english words. We really appreciated her efforts.

During the breaks we would get reacquainted with friends we new from China. We invited them to visit us on weekday evenings. Our house would become a meeting place of interesting characters that thought they knew everything. But the end result for all these discussions and arguments came to little consequence.

Our spiritual life, during this time was not compliant to the biblical teaching. Yet we felt we got along fine. Mrs Wiens started to receive our mail and would bring it over. This was the first writing and news I received since arrival. When I opened the letter, I recognized Step Dad's handwriting. And with apprehension I read about an unbelievable occurrence that should never happen to human beings.

Chapter 41

News

Dear John,

After receiving your letter from China, we waited until after the harvest and then took the train destined for Moscow. In the city of Kharkow the KGB asked us where we were going. When they found out that we were destined for Moscow, they ordered us off the train onto another one going back. We arrived eighteen miles short of our home. By now we were out of money and had to cover the distance on foot through rain and mud. Then we were compelled to walk another twelve miles to a loading place where a freight train was waiting. A large number of people were assembled and were all packed into these boxcars eighty in each. Every opening was sealed and the doors locked. By the lowering of the temperature we felt that the train was going in a northerly direction. The misery increased by the hour. There was not enough room to lie down. Everybody was in distress with no toilet facilities and no drinking water. There was one bucket in this car that served for waste. Once a day this container was emptied and without rinsing refilled with some thin grits as our meal. Because of the high, humidity inside the car and the very low temperature outside, every piece of metal and bolts protruding through the wooden wall were covered with ice. The occupants had to line up to get some moisture by licking the metal. This journey lasted over two weeks. By the time the train reached the destination, a number of children and older folks had died. No one had any knowledge of where we were going until the train stopped and those who survived had to walk a long distance to some barracks surrounded with barbed wire. These served as living quarters.

After orientation it was discovered that we were near the city of Vologda, about 200 miles northeast of Moscow. After a while we got acquainted with each other. There we were evangelical preachers, Catholic priests, rabbis, merchants, owners of property that ever had employed anybody, Christians, doctors and professors. In our dilemma we cried to God for help. If there is any possible way you can help us, we would appreciate it.

Your Dad J.J.

After reading this letter I set there a while stunned. It did not make any sense to me why all this had to happen. Just before I left home, Step Dad and I had a talk, about leaving together. He declined, giving a reason: "It can't get any worse."

Chapter 42

News

With the letter still on my lap, I prayed, "Lord, how can I help?" It was incredible that these innocent citizens, the prime of the land, were treated in such a manner. Coming out of my shock, I went to Mrs. Wiens and explained that all my loved ones were exiled and in a concentration camp. After a few moments she said; "Only God can help them; we must pray for them relentlessly."

I made further inquiries without stirring up any hopeful solution. The newspapers now were broadcasting the harshness of the Stalin regime. Our existence in the U.S.at present was difficult, yet hopeful in comparison with those in the Soviet concentration camps.

A few Sundays later some of the newcomers were received as members of the church including Henry and me.In the afternoon the whole group went joy riding. They showed us the Kings River Canyon and other noteworthy attractions. These afternoon outings were enjoyable and relaxing after reading Dad's letter. Many photographs and snapshots were taken and preserved. Anna,our housekeeper was in most of these and I liked this girl.

A different routine gradually developed in each of our lives on "M" street. After breakfast each went his own way. Anna would go to her sister and help her with the children, Henry and I would go into the business section of this little town. Occasionally we would meet a church member who was willing to talk with us. It was amazing how this industrialized country was faring. Coming together in the evening, Anna had the dinner ready and everyone enjoyed the meal and related some bits of happenings of the day.

I had a liking for Anna and the only way to find out if there was a responding attitude on her part was on our way to night school. She sat in the rear seat between Henry and me and, not having any prior experiences with girls, I did not know how to approach her. Dinner completed and dishes washed, Anna went to her room to get ready for the evening. While waiting for every one to go, I wrote on a piece of paper three crucial words, "I love you." I folded the paper and while sitting in the car, with her pressed it into the palm of her hand. All through the two hours of evening class there was not one inkling of a reaction to the note. I thought my attempt was a failure.

At bedtime Henry went and got his mattress. Next I stepped into that room to pick up my mattress, when Anna closed the door and asked me if I meant what I had written? I told her yes. She kissed me and said, "I too love you."

The ceiling was not the limit of my emotions. No girl ever kissed me like that. Immediately she opened the door not to arouse any suspicion and I walked out with my mattress. Next day we had decided to take a walk after dinner and consented to walk again on the following evening. Her two brothers did not like what was happening to their sister. Their intention now was to discourage Anna's and my relationship. They pictured the rosiest future for her and the possibility marrying a rich farmer's son. Their plan worked. Anna broke our relationship.

The following couple of weeks there were evangelistic services at our church conducted by a Rev.Schultz. The meetings were held in the spirit of expectation. A great many both young and older folk responded to the invitation to accept Christ as Lord and Savior. John Anna's brother, was also in this group. Now John realized the evil destructive part he had in black-balling me with his sister, and asked me to forgive him.I forgave. In the meantime Anna had gone to work for a family a few miles out of town as cook and children's companion. It was impossible for me to visit her.

The Friesen family had left their crippled son Abe, in China. Dad Friesen thought he might work out something in the U.S. with some friends who were in a position to put up a bond or guarantee that the son would not be a burden to the state. Although a number of citizens volunteered to furnish bond, it was to no avail. Abe was transferred by ship to Berlin, Germany,to a hospital. The daily expenses amounted to $70.00 per month that his dad had to put up. Anna's wages were forty dollars per month, five dollars she kept; the balance went towards Abe's expenses, the rest Dad had to put up.

After the orange harvest, sometime early in June, I took sick with fever. The man of the house thought perhaps it was the dreadful disease of meningitis that prevailed in this area. Mr. Martens, who also was my Sunday school teacher, was notified. After a few questions, he called a doctor who checked all my symptoms and established that I had malaria fever, Quinine was prescribed and I soon recovered. The five men on "M"street decided to dissolve their group so every one could be on his own.

Chapter 43
Communal Living

During the orange harvest we formed a closer bond of friendship with the Bergmann brothers, Henry and John. The younger one originally had provided passports for the Friesen family to cross the Amur river into China. They had rented an upper flat consisting of a large living room, closed in back porch, a swinging door between a wooden stairway leading to the outside, and an upper screened side porch which led into one single bath. John F. found someplace else to live. The four of us accepted the offer to move in with the Bergmann brothers. A young couple with a small child lived downstairs on the ground floor. The side of the house, plastered inside and stuccoed outside, faced the the street and was approximately seventy-five feet from the curb. It had a large parking area but no trees. The windows upstairs were all double hung and approximately three feet by four feet in size. One faced the street, the second south and the third the rear.

The furniture upstairs had one oblong three by five table with a single drawer that served as cash box for money and other valuables, two chairs and a small round wood stove. A Premus gasoline cooking stove sat on one end of the table with a handy one gallon can of fuel for the stove sitting somewhere on the floor.

Another man moved in by the name of John Bekker, a friend of the Bergmann brothers. Each of us had his own folding cot with bedding that were lined up along the outside wall of these two rooms. The Bergmanns had the priority on the stove and made use of it. The rest of us were on our own. Cleaning the house was not a big deal. The use of the bathroom in the morning created quite a problem. To avoid inconveniences and quarrels, I would get up before anyone else and not be in anyone' way.

We just had obtained a new work assignment on this particular day. It was a chilly night. As I got up and went to the bathroom, Henry Bergmann dressed only with his bathrobe, was stirring in the wood stove preparing to warm up the house. He did not notice any left over live coal from the previous night's fire. As usual after the wood was placed into the stove he would pour some gasoline onto it. Still holding the can in his hand the fumes in the stove exploded igniting the uncovered opening.

The poor man was so bewildered. Running to the window he thought he could fling the can outside. Not being able to open it, he ran back to the swinging door. Half way through he dropped the can short of the stairs. The gasoline was running down the steps between the cracks of the lower apartment all the way down and outside. A huge ball of fire and smoke engulfed the entire screened porch.

Opening the bathroom door I found myself trapped. Planning a way of escape through the tiny window of the bathroom was impossible.

Next thing I calculated was to open the door, kick the screen off its molding and lower myself down and fall the balance of the distance to the ground. All this happened in just a few seconds. While landing I fell so hard that I injured my left shoulder seriously. Outside I now could see the burning stairs, so I hollered fire a few times and knocked on the front door of the tenants. The man would not believe me. Coming outside he now looked and some of his belongings started to burn. They had a new sewing machine that he requested me to help him to carry outside. Than he went inside to help the family.

There was a commotion going on upstairs, the window was open and the table legs were showing, three men pushing and arguing how to get the table through the opening.

"Why don't you pull it back, remove the drawer and than toss it down," I suggested.

"The money will scatter was the reply."

I went to the side window where the drawer came down right side up, the few coins that scattered I picked up and put back into the drawer. In the meantime the fire department had arrived and with the extinguisher put out everything that was burning.

Not much structural damage was done except some electrical damage and the ceiling and walls were blackened. We stayed in this flat while it was refurbished. The very serious damage Henry sustained was on his left hand and face, but particularly to the lower part of his left foot. Medical treatment and the healing process tied him down and he was unable to work for eight months.

That morning we had to report to a new job. We arrived late which was against the company's rule. The second score against us was the excitement of the morning and loud talks were going on. Besides that my shoulder was in extreme pain. Our performance did not meet the foreman's approval and within two hours we were dismissed. I did not seek medical attention for the damaged shoulder which gradually quit hurting.

We all were restless. Discussions proved that some needed a change. Henry Lowen talked about going to Pennsylvania to some relatives, Henry Koslow desired more schooling particularly in Rochester,Bekker talked about going to New York. Loewen and Koslow teamed up and left for the east by car. Shortly after this Bekker also left.

This seasonal work was not adequate to sustain my interests.We had gone as far as Watsonville for the apple harvest,figs in Fresno,area and oranges in the surrounding towns. The language was an extreme barrier besides some manners I needed to acquire. I had no communication with Anna. Occasionally I would see her in church. There was nothing that held my attraction in Reedley.

Chapter 44

A Decision

After experiencing this state of mental evaluation, I went to praying the Lord for guidance and an open door. Rev. Hofer came to mind. I decided to pay him a visit. Perhaps he would know where a young man of my type could go to school and work his way through. After visiting his house one evening and explaining my desires and lack of funds, he said that our denominational school in Hilsboro, Kansas had no working opportunities. Biola would be the one that he would recommend. Many students there found helpful employment to sustain them.

He wrote for an application which arrived shortly. Reading it through a few times with the help of a dictionary, I filled out all questions except one: how will you pay your expenses?

Walking back to Rev. Hofer I showed him the filled out questionnaire and pointed out that I did not know what to say. I did not have any money. He suggested that I write in the Scripture passage Philippians 4:19, "But my God shall supply all your need according to His riches in glory by Christ Jesus." Having done this I felt encouraged and thanked him for the help. Mailing this this letter to Los Angeles, I wished something would become of this attempt.

The following week we had a call to report to pick oranges in the Realto area, east of Los Angeles. My concern about how we would receive our mail was needless. The Bergmanns had taken care of this detail and within two weeks I had an answer from the school that they wanted to interview me.

On Saturday I wondered what would be the best way for me to ghetto the school. The crew boss suggested I take the Red car that stopped at Seventh and Spring streets and that, if I wanted to go Sunday morning, he would take me to the car stop. This proposition was accepted.

All the way to the big city I had a good feeling that something eventful would happen. Arriving at the terminals, I asked my way around and walked the distance on foot. In the letter it said ask for Mr. Hale, the dean of men. Not knowing the difference between men's and women's dormitories, I walked into the women's foyer and requested to see Mr. Hale. The receptionist suggested the other entrance and, while she was explaining to me, the dean of women, talking to some lady, turned around and suggested that she could help me. After the introduction she made the offer to attend church, which was in progress now, and that she would introduce me to Mr. Hale later.

This was the famous Torrey Institute, a training center for young men and women from where great missionaries, teachers, pastors, preachers and evangelists had come. Miss Coulter who headed the women's dormitory, led me upstairs, and we were seated in the last seats in the center row of the balcony.

From there I faced straight ahead toward the pulpit and choir, an excellent observation point to see what was going on and the magnificent high ceiling structure of the Church of the Open Door. The first time in an English speaking worship service, made a lasting impression on me.

After the service Miss Coulter led me to the dining room where the students eat lunch and here I was introduced to Mr. Hale, the dean of men. In the dining room I met some familiar faces from the Reedley church; Rev. Eitzen's son, Jake and a few others. At least there was somebody that understood the German language with whom I could fluently communicate.

Lunch completed, Mr. Hale suggested that we go upstairs to his office for an undisturbed interview. Jake consented to come along to help with communications. Numerous difficulties and problems were laid bare, particularly the language problem. I then requested that if possible I attend classes and just mix with the students and learn this semester without credits. After a pause he consented and added that I should see Mr. Whitwell in charge of student employment. With prayer we were dismissed.

It was a wonderful day, a worthwhile experience, and I was grateful for the outcome of events. The Red car that brought me also took me back to Realto and from there I walked the distance to the apartment we stayed in. I explained to the crew boss my intention to quit Monday and, to please have my paycheck in the evening. He consented.

Chapter 45
Biola

Tuesday morning my boss took me out again to the Red car stop and with my few belongings I boarded the tram. When arriving at the men's dormitory, the desk clerk had no knowledge of my arrival since it was in the middle of the semester. He was puzzled. He questioned me and than called Mr. Hale and in a few minutes he showed a satisfactory face and led me to a vacant room with the instructions to come down for further instructions after getting settled.

Room and board were seven dollars per week which included three meals. I was requested to comply with all the student regulations and participate in all exercises voluntarily. In the dining room I was assigned to a specific table, where Jake Eitzen was the head. For table manners I observed others and did likewise. Since the sexes were mixed at the table, there was a lively conversation going on of which I at first understood very little. After the introduction several questions

Biola in Los Angeles

were asked. Jake helped to mediate to everyone's satisfaction.

With the familiarization of the curriculum and time table with help from other students, I was in control quickly.Making friends in this place was no problem. The difficulty was that everyone had to meet the grades and study was the priority.

Gradually it made sense to me that I was here to study spelled out in plain "work." Everything a student did I copied. Mr. Whitwell, dean of student employment, was approached. The only thing at present were jobs available to work in the restaurants that paid off in meals. On these assignments I stayed the balance of the semester. These meals were credited to me and I was excused from attending lunch and dinners at school. The morning classes were dismissed at eleven-thirty and a quarter to twelve. My job started as bus boy to carry food trays for elderly ladies. There were no classes in the afternoon.

Gradually my relationship with the students and faculty and navigating through the city improved except for my finances.

Two months before the graduation of the senior class,there was a note in my mail box to see the desk clerk. I had not been able to meet some of my obligations and there was now an amount outstanding that needed attention. He gave me one week to come up with money to balance the account.

The question that was on my mind now was if I was at the right place. Rehearsing one step after the other, I came to the conclusion that this was the Lord's leading and He had the supplies and would continue to guide my affairs. Through these few months there at the Institute, I heard a number of prayers being answered, students claimed victory of obsessing problems, and long prayer vigils were held for the school itself which was in dire need of finances. There was no letup of the depression now plaguing this country.

Chapter46
Help In Time

Monday after the second class I walked down the steps to the next session. I noticed Mr. Whitwell talking to some students who were pointing towards me. He than asked me if I would accept a job that required working half a night from six in the evening till midnight. I said yes. A graduating student was leaving after school and he would introduce me to the superintendent of this particular building that evening. The gentleman said he would accept the trade. What an answer to prayers! The job paid fifty-two dollars per month. I was paid half that amount every two weeks. I soon squared with the desk and things were normal. This was a definite answer to my prayer petition that I was not forsaken. The balance of the school term, I continued to attend the morning sessions, have lunch and then rest in the afternoon. Dinner was prepared in the form of a lunch that I ate at about seven-thirty at night with the rest of the maintenance crew.

These were the names of those who worked at night: the superintendent, Mr. Slater, stayed only till eight o'clock, Mr. Jones then had the oversight till midnight, Alex took care of individual offices and Otho, my partner from school. This was a thirteen story office called the Bartlett Building with thirteen floors and the basement that housed the individual machinery necessary to operate this complex. Three elevators and one fire escape stairs helped move the daily traffic. Our job consisted of taking the refuse from the restaurant on the third floor down the elevator and set it in the alley, sweep all halls and wash the hall floors with machines and mop them. It was essential that the use of the elevators required licensed operators. This we tended to immediately.

Because during the summer vacation students were not allowed to live in the dormitories, an outside apartment came in handy where several of us moved in. Walking outside just before closing the school, the dean of men met me and brought the good news that the faculty had accepted me as full fledged student for the next fall semester. A goal was in sight and some plans did formulate for which I was extremely happy.

Chapter 47
Visiting Friends

Jake Eitzen graduated, had gone home, and was going to be ordained and commissioned as a missionary to Africa. This I wanted to witness. Several professors of the Institute would be there to participate. Perhaps I might get a ride back. Saturday morning early the tram took me out to Highway 99 and there several motorists took me all the way to Reedley. Without notifying Aaron Langemann, I showed up. They gladly took me in and entertained me also for the night.

While attending the morning worship service in Reedley I made a comparison, of my former life here, and now the life in Los Angeles. I was thankful and happy the Lord had made it possible for me to be at Biola.

The ordination took place in the afternoon and the professors from Biola took part in this impressive ceremony. When they were ready to drive back to L.A., I approached them getting a ride back. After haggling among themselves they agreed to make room for one more passenger. Arriving in the city around midnight, I was let off near the Red car line thinking that one would be that way shortly and bring me closer to my destination. After a few hours of following the rails without seeing a single vehicle, I arrived in my apartment, tired, and glad to be able to rest.

Chapter 48
Learning is Work

The fall semester had signed in more students than the previous year. All unmarried students had to live in school dormitories. The married ones were exempted from this rule. To my delight the faculty had added the English class and deleted another one. This added another year to the subject I had to take. It was a two year course I would complete in three. Numerous things and requirements started to pile up. Somehow time had to be provided and some items abandoned. Approaching Mr. Hale about these things, he helped me to sort them out in order to have adequate sleep and study time. I would drop morning exercise and breakfast attendance, but not the eight-thirty devotional time every student had to attend. As a father to his sons, so was the dean of men to this group at this time. I gleaned real constructive admonitions, advice, and guidance I gleaned out of these sessions. The rest of the schedule was the same we had last semester.

Dean of men.

While on my way to work I stopped at the corner of the block to read the headlines of the newspapers. The depression was worldwide; Matchking of Sweden commits suicide, Mr. Kodak kills himself, executives in New York, Chicago and other cities were jumping to the street from high rise buildings. This was not a normal situation. At lunch time at work we had a discussion on this subject. Here I was questioned how bad the Russian situation was compared with ours?

I told them that while still in Reedley I received the first letter from my folks in Russia. A month later another came via New York, addressed to one of our distant relatives with the request to forward it to Mrs. Wiens' address. Evidently Dad was not sure if the KGB had let the first one through. In this second letter he bitterly complained about the severe hardships and austere treatments they all had been experiencing. If help would not come soon, there was a question of their survival. He mentioned that every morning they would find dead bodies outside the camp, people who could not make it to the barracks. The frost killed them. Since news ceased to come, I was of the conviction that they all either were killed or had not survived. Those were death camps.

The above news I related to these men. Most of the time our lunch hour was taken up with studying some of our school lessons. Coming to work we passed daily down of Sixth Street, Pershing Square, that took the entire block in. This place was filled with people that had nothing to do or were listening to agitators and soapbox speakers. These were difficult times for everybody.

While in the classroom, quite frequently Dr. White, the president of the school, would come down and request special prayers for the financial need of the institution. Whoever the lecturer was would suspend his lessons and the entire student body then remained in prayer. Individual members of this body, as they felt, led would rise to their feet and audibly voice their petitions to God, one after the other, both men and women. These were unforgettable moments that had some food for thought. Psalm 50:15, "Call upon Me in the day of trouble: I will deliver you, and you will glorify Me."

Sundays and holidays we did not work nor was there school. This time was taken to catch up on some important lessons. Occasionally some student came to my room to visit.Sunday nights I usually attended the Church of the Open Door that was sandwiched in between the two dormitories. Noted speakers always spoke in the evenings, but going to bed early was a treat. It was a privilege to be able to listen how these gifted men presented Biblical truth in their own individual way. Listening was also a learning process.

Holy days like Thanksgiving weekend would empty the school dormitories except for a few students of which I was one. Those were days when loneliness became an uncomfortable companion. Monday morning at our devotional, students were reporting some of their experiences of hitchhiking. On this particular morning Rev. Hale announced that a student by the name of Kraft had a fatal accident going home to his parents in Wasco. By next June he would have graduated. Serious thoughts and sympathy were expressed towards the family.

Chapter 49
Summer Vacation

The desire to visit old friends in Reedley helped me to formulate a plan of getting there by way of hitchhiking. The next long weekend off from work and school was in the spring. On this particular day the Red car provided a ride past Glendale to Highway 99. A young man traveling north picked me up and drove me past the mountain ridge. The conversation was cordial and on the subject of why I studied at Biola. He expressed his regrets of not being able to take me any farther.

Before venturing on this journey I had prayed for mercy and grace to express my belief and conviction of man's moral and spiritual responsibilities according to what the Bible taught. So far I had no problem in expressing myself, although I was weak on the language side. The next ride was with a middle-aged gentleman in an older pickup. Our conversation had the same approach and sensing my difficulties with the language I explained that my residence in the U.S. was only in its second year. He also related his participation in World War 1 which led me to ask him of his close calls having faced death. Sensing that he never had taken to heart the army chaplain's admonitions, I read John 3:16 to him " For God so loved the world, that He gave His only begotten Son, that who so ever believes in Him should not perish but have everlasting life." No sooner had I finished reading this passage then the man got extremely angry and rough. We soon came to a side road. He then ordered me out and proceeded going west from Highway 99. All shaken up I reviewed what possible wrong was done that could have been avoided so as not to offend him. I concluded that he was not angry at me but with God. Prayer is the best spirit calmer and guide in difficult circumstances, proven in the past and also now twenty miles from Bakersfield. Not knowing the person's name or address, it was almost one hundred percent certain that our paths never would cross again, but two years later they did under very unusual circumstances.

Several autos had passed and then a two seater stopped. A middle-aged lady invited me to step in. She addressed me by saying that traveling by oneself was not fun and I looked like I could entertain her since there were no radios in those days. How delighted she was when I related to her that I was a student at Biola. When she discovered that my destination was Reedley, she added that Visalia was her hometown. By now we arrived in Bakersfield, and stopped at a hotel restaurant. She added that we should have lunch before we went on. The Lord not only provided comfort but relief and lunch. Thank you, Lord!

The afternoon conversation as we traveled was church related. Interested in my experiences she prodded me on to reveal more of what had happened to my folks and the politics in Russia. Arriving at Airport Boulevard I thanked her for the graciousness and for the lunch again and we parted. It was sunset before I reached my destination, Aaron's home.

Visiting in Reedley was refreshing and relaxing. I was brought up to date on many events. Likewise I exchanged how my life was in Los Angeles that I was working nights and studying in the day time. The subject of the indebtedness to the Aid Society that advanced the hundred and twenty dollars to come across the Pacific Ocean came into conversation and that there at present was a need to help others.

Monday morning early Aaron drove me on Kingsburgh to Highway 99, where I caught a ride back to the city. The first leg was up to the top of the mountains. The gentleman had some business there and I walked some distance and was waiting to be picked up by another traveler. A vehicle with several men in it slowed down and one shouted, "What is your name?"

I did not know what to think of this type of approach. They drove on about twenty yards. One got out and walked towards me, when about fifteen feet away he looked and then shouted: "It is not him," and walked back. It was a puzzle that I could not solve. Could it be that they were some detectives or were looking for a missing person that I resembled? Another car offered me a ride up to the tram that brought me home.

Another school year had passed and also relief from studies, but I was glad for the job that in this scarcity of work provided the needed income. My partner at work and I rented a one room apartment during the summer, made our own meals and cared for personal obligations. A student friend from school invited me on one summer afternoon to drive with him to Santa Monica to have a swim in the ocean. I enjoyed the swim but did not like the cold current of ocean water that chilled me to the point of chattering teeth. Never again did I go out to swim in the ocean.

Since my finances were improving, I decided that it would be to my advantage to remove my indebtedness the of one hundred twenty dollars I owed to the Aid Society. Monthly money orders were purchased and mailed to Hillsboro, Kansas. Little did I realize that this would cause an amazement at the Mennonite conference when the treasurer read the balance of the outstanding funds and then added that a student at Biola was making monthly payments to reduce his debt.

Fall semester had come and many new and older students had enrolled from various parts of the nation. Also new personnel were added to the school staff. One gentleman by the name of Hillis came from WallaWalla, Washington; the students named him "Daddy Hillis." This gentleman was in charge of drumming up finances for the school. Changes had been made. The men's dormitory half had been leased to a hotel chain who were now operating the upper six stories as a hotel and the school the lower four for students. Meeting Mr. Hillis in his office one day, I had to tell him my experiences about which he was genuinely interested. He also related that he quit his job as state warden for WallaWalla prison and was trying to help Biola. His twin sons and a nephew also were enrolled.

Chapter 50

Anna

In the mean time I had joined a small church that required a street car ride fifteen minutes from school. The track ran right by Sixth Street so there was little walking. People were friendly and cordial. Some had invited me to their home. I liked their fellowship.

Shortly before Easter I received a card from Anna wishing me a delightful holiday. Without hesitation I replied and expressed my appreciation for the greetings. A week later she replied, describing her work for the family who employed her. It was obvious that I still loved her. With this in mind the next letter was written accordingly. The response was unmistakable: that girl still loved me.

Immediately I started to plan how and when I might see her. The next holiday with a weekend off was Memorial Day in May, and that is when I could take off extra time to hike up to Reedley. Letters kept coming and going regularly which helped my spirit at school. I was looking forward to accomplishment with greater enthusiasm.

Early Monday morning I was standing on the highway going north and in no time someone picked me up. Arriving in Kingsburg, I had to walk all through town and some on the road to Reedley. The sun was hot and I had no hat and since this stretch had few autos going that way, it was evident that walking might bring me there by late evening. Since I had no watch it was a guessing game to tell the time of the day. A gentleman brought me the last several miles into town near sunset. Aaron and his wife entertained me again. On telling him the purpose of my visit, he volunteered to take me to Anna's place of employment. Anna had explained our relationship to the lady employer. So she had graciously absented the entire family and had gone to Fresno for an evening of entertainment and left the entire house to us. Aaron said he would wait while I visited until I was ready to leave. After nearly two hours of a delightful visit, I parted leaving with more information about her family affair: the brother in Germany and also about her brother John, who had married had a little son and had lung cancer. It was sad that a young father was stricken with this deadly disease. No promise could be made when the next visit would be. However we promised each other to write. The next morning Aaron delivered me again to the nearest point of getting a ride back to Los Angeles and by evening I had arrived home.

Chapter 51
Travel for the Cause of Biola

The frequent visits with Mr. Hillis brought new evidences to light that he was on some kind of planning for the purpose of raising some revenue for the Institute. Now he unveiled it. He had selected four students to comprise one team touring southern California and another team of four students touring the United

Gospel Team.

States and Canada. He asked if I would be willing to join the second group. He then went on to explain that this team would be selected from students of different nationalities.

Then he named them: Jitsu Morikava from B.C., Canada; Daniel Schirmer, a Hopi Indian; Andrew Dercher, a Yugoslavian; John Thielmann from Russia; and Lloyd Blackwell from California, whose father would furnish the automobile. He then proceeded to outline the itinerary and conditions. No salary is promised. From what churches would provide, first the traveling expenses would be paid. What is left over would be divided equally among the five. At least one hundred meetings were scheduled for the entire summer. We would leave when school was out, take the southern route to cover Arizona, New Mexico, Colorado, Oklahoma, Nebraska, go as far as Ohio and Indiana, and then the northern route covering the states to the Pacific coast, north into British Columbia, down through Washington, Oregon, California and then home.

Quite frequently I had wondered how a soft spoken person like Mr. Hillis could have been a warden of a penitentiary. This question I addressed to him. His answer came strong and determined, "I got fed up with that kind of life where I had to treat men like animals; that's why I retired and volunteered for this work here at Biola where I can help build young lives for Christ."

This was a very resolute man and so was the entire staff of this institution to stick by a school that was financially in serious difficulties. I weighed the problems of leaving my job and then getting it back when we returned. Mr. Hillis assured me that they would do everything possible to arrange these conditions. Next I was interested if it would be feasible to arrange a meeting at the church in Reedley when we returned through California. He answered it was in the planning. I accepted this proposition on condition that Mr. Slater release me for the summer. In the evening I explained what had been proposed to me and whether the school would vouch for satisfactory reinstatement. He said, "John I would love to have you back next fall."

Gratefully I accepted this assurance.

Mrs.Dennis, one of the teachers in child education, who had a Bible class on Sunday mornings at the Church of the Open Door, invited us five students scheduled for this cross country trip to be present at the opening part of her class. We were introduced and she instructed this body to keep us on their daily prayer list as Biola had attached an important significance to this particular team.

Mrs. Anna Dennis.

Putting all our belongings into storage, we took only the very necessary clothes needed. The departure was scheduled for a Monday morning in front of the dormitory. Parked outside stood an old Pontiac sedan with an attached trunk. Alongside stood Lloyd and his father, the senior Blackwell, we four boys, Mr. Hillis and Dr.White, the president of the school. He gave us the charge and than prayed for us. Mr. Hillis handed an envelop to Lloyd with our itinerary and instructions. He told us to be sure to ask at each stop for the mail that contained further scheduled meetings ahead of us.

Chapter 52
The Team

Now was the time to get closer acquainted. We had seen each other in various classes but never had a meaningful conversation. Lloyd started to tell us that his dad loaned their family car for Biola's need for the summer. It was a real sacrifice on the family's part. His sister Doris had graduated that spring and was looking forward to going as a missionary to Africa. I had met her at the dinner table several times. Lloyd's height was about five foot ten, his dark hair combed back. He was in control with his expressions when telling a joke. Only after every body had his fill of laughter would he smile.

Jitsu, about twenty years of age born of Japanese parentage in the Vancouver, British Columbia, Canada area, spoke a very beautiful english, and was about five feet tall with a narrow face and light complexion. He spoke highly of the young people of the Baptist Church where he was a member.

Andrew Dercher's age was about twenty-four, five foot eight inches tall, medium large build. His face featured strong cheek bones with large proportionately spaced dark brown eyes. The dark brown hair wasn't too plentiful that covered his head, but there was no sign of baldness. The straight nose on the flat side was crossed below by a thin lipped mouth and double chin. His handicap was clubbed feet. His eyes did not blink too often and, when he spoke, the face had a sad expression.

According to Andy's testimony he was born in Yugoslavia of illegitimate parentage. His mother married a man that hated this kid. At every opportunity if no one was around, he would ether trip or kick him. One spring day Andy was playing near a flowing ditch full of water, when his Step dad passed and gave the child a push into the water and kept on walking. The grandmother had seen all this and opening the window, she shouted, "You better pull that child out or you will be in trouble."

Reluctantly he complied and Andy was rescued. This kind of life was tolerated until age fourteen when grandma decided to send Andy to Oregon in the U.S.A. to one of her relatives.

Because of the aunt's persistence Andy received some public schooling. At age eighteen he ventured to Hollywood, learned some dancing and made his living by performing in public.

Somehow he got involved with some cults which he thought would satisfy his spiritual quest for the mysterious hereafter. A chance meeting with a student from Biola aroused Andy's curiosity to visit the Church of the Open Door where he got an earful that brought him back again. He experienced inner healing and deliverance from decades of hatred and fears by openly confessing Christ as his Saviour and breaking ties with how he was living and with his old friends.

After Andy's enrollment in school, he shared his life with some students who prayed for him. Loving and praying for his parents, who in the meantime also had immigrated to Oregon, was a new experience for him. Letters were exchanged with his mother and the desire to meet her became an obsession. When he discovered that we would pass the town his parents lived in on the way down from Canada, his joy knew no bounds.

Daniel Shermer was about five foot six, had a typical Indian red complexion, brown eyes,unruly hair, a short neck,and had a strong muscular physique. His face was pleasant, friendly and relaxed. We inquired about this unusual name for an Indian. He then related this amazing story:

The Hopi Indian belief is that when a child is born and the mother dies during childbirth, the infant is the killer and therefore must be destroyed. In his case his mother died during childbirth. The father now intended to destroy his little son. Miss Schermer, a single lady missionary and also a R.N., who had assisted in this difficult delivery, requested to raise this child as her own. Because he was rescued from certain death, she named him Daniel. As a child he became very attached to his foster mother. She trained him in all the Christian principles. Early in life Daniel understood what salvation through Christ meant. Although his father cared very little about him, Daniel, knowing the history of his being with the missionary as a son, loved his father also. Through him he learned many of the Indian traditional habits, customs, and traditions. In school he obtained the proper education.

When we arrived at the Hopi reservation, Daniel introduced us to his missionary mother and the real father. There was also an older brother by the name of John whom we did not get to meet. Daniel spoke of him as being often in difficulty with the law.

In our itinerary Mr. Hillis had provided extra time to be at Daniel's home and also other sites that he thought we would enjoy visiting. On the way to Colorado, the Grand Canyon was a stopping point. It truly was a marvelous sight to see this grand carving through the mountains. Not having had exercise we decided to walk down the trail instead of paying for a mule ride. About two-thirds down we made a turn around and started to walk up hill. Needles to say I almost did not make it. Arriving on top we all lay down and rested for some time. From here we proceeded to our next meeting.

The format of the meetings were all the same. The training of young people at Biola and the need for finances and students was explained. The balance of the time was taken up for personal testimony by each member of the team. They were well attended. Through the offerings and contributions we realized that the depression was hard on everyone.

The itineraries were well planned and the meetings properly spaced for us to be there on time. At each mail drop I could expect a letter from Anna. All her letters were addressed to Biola and Mr. Hillis included all private correspondence in his package to the team. Never did I delay to answer her letters.

The scheduled appointments led us through the Royal Gorge and Pike's Peak, points of interest not to be forgotten. Occasionally we had a mix up with dates, we were at the end of our schedule and the dispatched package had not arrived. This happened in Nebraska,

After we ran out of appointments, five precious days were lost until by persuasion Lloyd finally sent a telegram to Mr. Hillis. The reply came back that we had missed three appointments, and were to go to the next one.

When arriving at the next meeting place, we found a very distraught pastor informing us that they were assembled last night. A large crowd had waited till nine-thirty. Since this was harvest time and our arrival already was late today, we departed for the next appointment. This was a lesson to be alert for these types of problems. It did not happen again. Meetings were scheduled through Indiana and then up to Chicago, through Wisconsin and the northern route back to the Pacific coast.

On one of our meetings in Wisconsin an elderly childless couple had invited us to stay overnight at their house. The lady was very talkative, mostly dwelling on her personal experiences of being followed by strangers. When we parted, she handed each one a five dollar gold piece. A Nebraska farmer while staying on his farm a couple of days also handed each one a silver dollar piece. These were the only financial benefits,we brought home. We were grateful for the generosity of that couple. While traveling we discussed the bizarre experiences of the lady. Some thought she may have had a persecution complex.

Chapter 53

We Have a Great God

Staying overnight at a students home in Seattle, I accidentally sprained my right ankle while walking outside. It swelled up with terrific pain. While speaking that evening, my body rested only on one foot. Jitsu sitting in back noticed that and after the meeting he asked what was wrong with my foot. I then related to him the incident that happened before the meeting.

From Seattle we went up across the Canadian border to Vancouver area where we had appointments in several churches including the one where Jitsu was a member. He was not aware that when he returned to Canada, he needed a new permit to enter the U.S. Was he shocked when the news reached him! Mrs. Dennis of the Bible study group that prayed for us daily discovered that we were now in Canada. She realized Jitsu's problem, and asked the group to pray while she went to the telephone. She called a friend of hers, the wife of an immigration officer, and related to her the problem. She then requested that she be kind enough to intervene in Jitsu's problem. The lady said she would. In a few hours this matter was cleared up and we were notified of clear sailing back. We found out that while we had traveled together these few months, prayer was our constant companion and now again help came before we realized it.

Several meetings were held down the coast until we arrived in Portland. Andy now alerted Lloyd to be sure and not miss the house where his mom and step dad lived. Lloyd stopped at the desired address and told Andy he had only fifteen minutes. Andy ran up the stairs to the porch and then knocked. An elderly lady opened the door. Seeing him she exclaimed "Andrew!" and then both fell in each other's arms. It took a full hour before he reappeared all in tears, jumped in, and while we started to move, both waved to each other until they could not see each other.

It took quite a while before Andy spoke up and told us that the reason it took so long was that he had to explain to his mom who Jesus was, what was accomplished on the Cross, that Christ already died for our sins, and that she needed to believe that and receive Him. She did. Andy was happy for the visit, although he did not see his step dad. When we arrived in Reedley late in the afternoon after many stops, I requested permission from Lloyd to use his car to go and visit Anna. It was a real delight to see her again. This time we talked about the serious business of getting married. She agreed on this venture for life wholeheartedly. In the meantime her parents had moved to Paterson, a few hours drive from Reedley towards San Francisco. She took it upon herself to notify her dad about our intention. I suggested that Thanksgiving weekend would be the appropriate time for me to come and we together would drive up to her Dad's place and I would make the formal request for his daughter in marriage. We parted happily with these decisions.

Since the Reedley church was one of the largest on the Pacific coast and well attended, we received a good reception and a generous offering that brought the expenses out of the red. On this last leg home Lloyd informed us that all the money given to us had gone for fuel and sundry travel expenses. While the depression was hard on all farmers, his dad and mom particularly were in dire need of assistance. He had sent home small amounts of money that went to cover the use of the vehicle as they had agreed.

Chapter 54

Back Home in School

We arrived at the Institute on time to sign in for a room, arrange our belongings and go to bed. The following day I went to see Mr. Hillis, whom the other students had informed about all happenings and finances. Since he knew each student had come home with only six dollars and one coin was a five dollar piece, he asked if I was going to keep it. I told him it would have to be spent. So he handed me five paper dollars in exchange for the gold coin. In the evening I visited the place of employment and found Mr. Slater and reported that I was back and able and willing to work again. The transition was made smoothly and thanks to the other student that held the job open for me.

Mr. Hillis told us four students to report to Mrs. Dennis' Bible class Sunday morning about nine. She and the entire group were glad to see us back healthy and in one piece with no accidents. Each one of us received an envelope containing ten dollars. We thanked them for their love and prayers. Mrs. Dennis thought a great deal of us four young men. Like a mother she kept us together by arranging Sunday afternoon appointments in various churches in Los Angeles and surrounding cities. She personally drove us in her two door Studebaker with seats in the rear. Three in the back seat was a crowd.

Chapter 55

Marriage Contemplated

Sometime later I found out that the faculty had a policy for students not to marry during school terms. This posed a problem for me. So in order to be certain of it, I made an appointment with Mrs.Dennis to have lunch in the cafeteria. Here I presented my problem to her. Since I had no home, no relatives, and no where to go during the holidays, my desire was to get married. I added that my desire was for Anna to know what this institution taught and that she attend as a visitor. She thought for awhile and then suggested that she would present this to the faculty. If the faculty would not permit it, I had to promise to obey. I promised. A few days later she sought me out and notified me permission granted.

Now how to find a way to Reedley?

Walking on Sixth street I noticed a sign in the window, "Will take passengers any where for a small fee." I walked in and asked how much to Reedley.

He asked,where is Reedley. I told him it is 25 miles east of Fresno. He had a passenger going to Fresno in the morning the fee is $5.00 and if I wanted to go along, be here at 8:00 a.m. I accepted this offer.

Anna had written that when I came this time I was to stop at her aunt's place where I could share the room with her older brother, Henry. He would take us to Paterson to her father's place the next day.

I arrived at dinner time and after greeting all, we sat down to dine. Many events and news were related including that her brother, John, with family were living at Dad's place also. After we were by ourselves, Anna told me that she had explained to her father of our intent to get married. He suggested that from that time on, she did not need to contribute to the brother's need in Germany. We also decided the most appropriate date for our wedding would be between semesters on December twenty-seventh.

The following day we arrived at the Friesen farm. Greetings were exchanged including the ill brother, his wife, Tina, with their little infant, Johnny. The sick brother faced surgery in the near future. Recovery was not guaranteed. Dad Friesen appreciated our coming and after we were by ourselves, I formally presented our wishes to get married and my request to receive his blessing. Questions like how and where we would live were asked. Things were satisfactorily answered. Mom had prepared a little snack with coffee. Dad had given us his blessings. Now we were ready to go back.

Some planning had to be done before the wedding. This we talked about. I mentioned things I would do in preparing an apartment. She mentioned that on her part the wedding expenses and the preparation were all hers. No help could be expected from anyone. Reasons were given that did not seem logical to me.

Next morning I went to the Greyhound Bus depot and purchased a return trip back to Los Angeles. So far I had not neglected any studies either in the subjects of the Bible or in the English except in the expression, in pronunciation, and in the formulation of proper sentences. It required hard labor and a will to succeed. Shortly before Christmas the dean of men, Mr. Hale, called me into his office and showed me my record as far as my room is concerned. He said, "I have only one black mark against you. I found your lights on after ten p.m. on one Sunday. That one I have erased. Your record at the dormitory is perfect."

"To be honest Mr.Hale," I said, "I have been working nights. It would be after midnight when I come in. Light is needed to prepare for the night."

Mr. Hale looked at me and said, "I mark only what I find at the checking time." I thanked him.

Chapter 56
Wedding

Christmas and wedding time approached. Students planned to visit someone or their home. Andy said he wanted to go up to Oregon and visit with the family. I also was looking for an apartment and made a deposit on one about twenty minute walking time from school.

This time I took the bus up to Reedley and walked to Aunt Susie's. Anna was there working busily. Henry took us to Fresno to get our marriage license. Next stop was the photographer. Several sittings had to be taken. The day had arrived, December twenty seventh. This was also the day my father had

Wedding.

passed away in 1920 during a typhoid epidemic in Russia.

This is a stark truth unless I build my home on solid ground. I wanted the Lord to bless my marriage. Sharing these thoughts with Anna, they were also her desire.

Anna now mentioned the wedding program. Aaron had drummed up a quartet, a friend of hers would sing a solo, Rev. Hofer had a sermon, and Rev. Eitzen would perform the nuptials. It sounded good to me. She also had invited many guests from the church. The entire preparation and setting she did with the help of a few friends. This was to be our day, never to be forgotten. This house had a foundation that stood the test of time. We promised till death us do part. Dad Friesen with his family were present, except the sick brother in Patterson and the one in Berlin, Germany. After the wedding, when we were by ourselves, I asked if Dad had paid the expenses. Anna told me she did. It was quite an elaborate feast. Having the knowledge of a seamstress, she made her own bridal outfit.

While still in China with the uncertain possibility of emigrating anywhere, Anna's Dad sent her to a school sponsored by a company that sold Singer sewing machines to learn machine embroidery. He also bought one machine and brought it along to America. The sewing machine was the only thing Anna got from her Dad.

The day after our wedding, Henry and I loaded all of Anna's belongings including the gifts and left for our new home in Los Angeles. Anna liked this apartment, which had one bedroom with a hideaway bed, a kitchen, and a bathroom. Only a few things that were needed for household use we unpacked. The remainder as left packed.

School did not begin until after the New Year, but I assumed my job responsibilities immediately. Walking for Anna was a problem. Most of the ambulating she ever did was inside a house. Now it posed a problem. Eventually things got adjusted and we managed to get there on time. It did not take long for me to discover that my wife was an excellent cook. I asked her how she got along by herself while I was at work? "No problem," she said; "I write letters and chat with my loved ones via mail."

To set up housekeeping was somewhat of a problem for not having a clothesline to dry the laundry. Off we went to hunt for an apartment where that convenience existed. A two story apartment at the base of a hill with a flat roof had this arrangement. Although it was quite a bit older and we had to climb to the top floor, Anna liked it better. My partner at work owned a '27 Chevy sedan. Together with his help we relocated. Eventually I had introduced my bride to most of the faculty and friends. Relentlessly Mrs.Dennis made speaking appointments for our team, which posed quite an inconvenience for me and Anna. I would not leave Anna by herself at home and coming with us made it very crowded. After a few tries, I gave it up and found I was able to arrange the time for more profitable study. In the church Anna was embraced warmly and made many friends.

Chapter 57
The Earthquake

On April ninth, I walked to work as usual, arriving a little before six in the evening. No sooner had I entered the office where our lockers were and Otho had changed his working attire then a violent earth movement swayed the entire structure up and down and sideways. The five gallon drinking water bottle on the stand was on the verge of falling over. Giving support to this fragile object and seeing Otho climbing on to the window sill ready to jump down, with a loud voice I said, "What are you trying to do?"

He looked back, his face white as a sheet, with the building still rolling and cracking as if it were breaking up. He came down.

Since the only elevator in operation after five thirty was stuck between floors in the shaft, a gentleman came running down the stairs. He stopped on the second floor where we were and asked Mr. Jones if he would go up to the fifth floor and get his hat. He obliged. A passenger from the tenth floor stepped into the elevator, the doors shut, and as soon as it started to move down, the emergency brakes froze the movement of the cage between floors. The movement in the elevator was extremely violent. The operator, a believer in Bible, thinking the end of the world had come, fell to his knees and prayed, "Lord take me up."

The passenger shouted, "Take me down."

The engineer on duty, seeing that the elevator was stuck between floors, walked the stairs to the floor above the elevator, opened the door, stepped onto the cage, and released the emergency brakes. Hearing all the commotion going on inside, he opened the trapdoor and told the operator not to move until he got off. He was the eye witness that related this incident.

Fear controlled us all. For about half an hour we did nothing. But then we were compelled to resume what we usually did. Starting from the top floor, we noticed after every few minutes the movement of the earth was much more noticeable here on top. It was a scary experience. The whole building seemed moved from side to side, twelve to thirty-six inches. The work was done in time.

Coming home later than usual, I found Anna very upset She

was glad to see me alive. Through all this excitement she had made several attempts to telephone the building in which I was employed, but failed. She was overjoyed. Rest and sleep were priorities. To bed we went. About every twenty to thirty minutes the after shocks had their devastating effect and the old rickety building prolonged the shaking, adding to our sleeplessness. Toward morning it finally subsided.

Considerable damage was revealed throughout the earthquake area,but none to Biola except minor cracks. Several deaths were reported. Coming from school I noticed a switchman sitting at the railroad tracks. A question addressed to him weeks later revealed that his wife died during the quake.

Some times in May Anna felt nauseated and did not desire to get out of bed. Not knowing what could be the matter, I went to the school doctor for some remedy. He explained that she was pregnant. Revealing this to Anna, she smiled and added, "I could have told you that."

Reading and listening I discovered a clinic only a few minutes from school by street car that specialized in gynecology. It's worth investigating. The whole plan, prenatal and delivery was one hundred and ten dollars and I could pay it on a time plan ten dollars per month. This was the best option available and I accepted it.

A letter went off to her folks informing them about new developments. After the close of school one week end Dad and Mom showed up. We were glad to see them. Not having an extra bed we sacrificed ours and slept on the kitchen floor the two nights they were with us. Satisfied that their daughter was happy, they left.

Chapter 58
The Lord is in Control

Periodically towards the summer I took Anna for a check up which turned out to be normal with the exception that her blood was on the anemic side and the doctor prescribed food rich in iron.

Going to church one Sunday morning, we had arrived and were entering the building when Anna fainted and nearly hit the porch decking. Calling for help, several ladies responded and carried her in the adjacent room where she soon recovered. Never again did she faint.

The men of the church asked for volunteers to come and help out to conducting gospel services at the Lincoln Heights jail on a particular Sunday, in the early afternoon. Only once had I gone to that prison with a group of students, but this time I went along. Arriving at the prison a number of other groups from other churches had arrived and were now entering the main room for assignment to different cells. We were going up to the second floor and were entering the elevator. As soon as I had entered and turned to face the door, a man came running towards me and stared as if he wanted something from me. After the completion of the service, as I was coming down the same elevator, the man was waiting for me. He asked if I recognized him, but I didn't. He then said, "I am the one that you quoted John 3:16 to on the way while hitchhiking with me two years ago and I had so rudely ordered you out of the car."

I now remembered! He continued, "After I left you off, an indescribable misery came over me. Coming home I had no rest nor peace. After some time I called a preacher and he helped me to find forgiveness by faith in the Lord Jesus Christ. Ever since I have been telling others what has happened to me."

This was a most unusual revelation to me, that this man recognized me. He did not know my name, nor did I know his. The way I felt was that the Lord brought us together for me to know that He is in control. I had the same suit on that day I had then and that is how he could have recognized me. Gratefully I have accepted this wonderful revelation: God is the heart changer.

A letter from Dad Friesen revealed that John was taken to San Francisco, had surgery, and died while the operation was in process. We attended the funeral and came right back. A short time later another letter explained that brother Abe in Berlin, Germany, had died. He was the nearest in the family to Anna and they had shared thoughts and plans together. Our photographs and letters were returned describing and picturing our wedding.

Shortly after Thanksgiving, sitting in the classroom, I experienced a sharp pain in the right side of the lower abdomen. Wasting no time, the school doctor sent me to the county hospital for a check up. They decided the appendix had to be removed as soon as possible. Reporting back to the infirmary at school, I discovered that the school paid for the hospital, but the student paid the physician. Emily, the nurse spoke up and said, "Let me talk to my physician I worked with last, he might do it."

A telephone call was made and he had agreed to do it only in the Pasadena hospital.

I left the name of the hospital and address with Anna. Arrangements at the work place were made to have a substitute and the following day towards evening I signed in at the hospital. After the surgery next morning, the tonsils were also removed on the second morning. Anna came to visit me once; friends from the church had brought her. Mr. Whitwell from school came after four days and he took me to the school infirmary for another two days. Things did not look good for me financially. Heavy thoughts raced through my mind. We could not last another month without additional income. We decided that an alternative solution was to move to Anna's sister near Merced. Christmas approached. The baby was due sometime in February and a decision had to be made.

I walked to the dean of the school and explained my situation to him. There was no alternative for me. He asked how much more time was left to graduate. I told him only six months. He asked if the Lord would provide funds for me to overcome the two months to convalesce would I return. I said I would.The address where we planned to go was taken.

In the meantime we had bought a 1927 four door sedan in running condition for seventy-five dollars. The roof needed replacement,but it would take us where we wanted to go. The belongings we had were still packed. They all went inside the small car. The sister was advised of our situation and she welcomed us to stay at her house for a few days till we knew what we had in mind to do.

The twenty sixth of December a letter from the president of the school arrived. In this letter it stated that someone was willing to put up the necessary money if I would return. We counselled together on this subject. We already had paid for the delivery of the newborn soon to come and my health would be improved ready to go to work in another month. We agreed to leave the next day which was our anniversary date. This Christmas we had at least someone of the family circle to exchange thoughts of peace on earth.

The trip was uneventful until we crossed the peak of the hills. There the overcast sky opened and streams of water poured down which slowed down our driving considerably. I had to navigate between rolling rocks and just prayed that none would hit us. The car roof did not hold the rain out; first it leaked on Anna's side and then on mine. Late that night we arrived at a friend's house who gave us shelter for the balance of the night. The next morning we ventured house hunting and found a nice cottage near a bakery and closer to school than we had lived previously. The price was affordable, Anna liked it, and we settled in. We were delighted to discover another young couple who attended Biola living in this court.

Next day with the letter in hand I walked up to the dean's office. He remembered the writing and said, "I am delighted that you came back so soon. Let's go to the treasurer's office."

There he explained that I was to draw weekly as much as I needed up to seventy five dollars. The Lord again had provided! What a wonderful provider He is. Psalm 103 is so fitting in our situation.

Chapter 59

Back in School

Having missed classes, I got assignments from different teachers which were not difficult to catch up except the psychology lesson I nearly did not pass on that.

Having drawn only sixty dollars, I went back to work.Being out of work for nearly two months, my body had to get accustomed to this type of movement. After a few evenings I was in good shape.

It was getting closer to Anna's delivery time. The obstetrician had predicted a normal birth which would be about the middle of February,give or take a few days. On the seventeenth in the evening, contractions began and a little later she lost the fluid. I rushed her to the clinic. There they thought it would take quite a while yet. Since one of the elevator operator wanted to take off on Sunday, he requested me to substitute as I had promised. For ten hours of work I get ten dollars. I needed it then. Early Sunday I went to the clinic and Anna informed me we had a daughter. I was glad she felt happy about it.

I had to be on the job before seven A.M. and monitor visitors all day until five p.m. After that I went to see Anna again. This time she nursed our child. We named her Anna Marie. In a few days I brought mother and child home. It is amazing how a child changes all priorities in a home. Mother and child had a few more checkups before graduation.

Before all of the group that had traveled together dispersed from school, we made inquiries about Andy's father. He then told us the following experiences: going home for Christmas he was prepared to communicate with his step dad who was not feeling very well. He told him that he had forgiven him the past and presented to him what Scripture teaches about forgiveness: "Father, forgive us as we forgive others," "those who believe in His name have eternal life," and many other quotations from Scripture. Andy told us he was happy to report that Step dad had become a changed man. It is amazing that children of God bear godly fruit, love and forgiveness. Children of darkness carry on with hatred, deception, lying and murder, etc. We were happy with Andy about the change in relationship with his family.

Daniel dated a girl also from the Hopi tribe. She was quite

a few years older but a very nice lady. I was casually acquainted with his brother, John, who was attending school.

Jitsu left for another school of higher learning.

Lloyd went back to San Dimas, his home town.

The Depression was easing off somewhat. We had a new president who also ordered all banks to get off the gold standard. Several work projects were in the making. This was June of 1934 which concluded with my graduation from three and a half years of very hard, diligent studying, plus earning a living and acquiring a family, all in the metropolis of Los Angeles. We dare not to stay here any longer than we had to.

With the greatest amazement I recall the experiences. On the application for admission to Biola. I quoted Philippians 4:19, "But my God shall supply all your need, according His riches in glory by Christ Jesus." This actually was fulfilled in my stay there at Biola. Praise His Holy Name!

Chapter 60

After

We had written our brother-in-law, Henry Toews, Anna's sister Elizabeth's husband, that we were graduating and coming up that way. He was farming with Kadota figs grown mostly for canning but also dried for human consumption. Henry took it upon himself to rent on our behalf some acreage of already standing trees with a crop on them to be harvested the coming August. Also, Dad Friesen, with his sons, Nick and George, had acquired acreage on the same terms. This acreage had a small house on it that we were able to rent and moved in. This small town called Planada ten miles east of Merced on the Yosemite highway was comprised of a fruit cannery, related supply stores, and farmers. It had a small abandoned church in which we, with the help of others, held Sunday school for children and adults.

The farmer's life in this community in summer time was a frustrating and demanding life, particularly at harvesting time with the fruit. Since the Kadota fig was a canning item, it had to be picked,graded, and shipped the same evening to Richmond. Local canneries would not put them up because there was no local demand. The over ripened ones were sulfured, sundried, and trucked to packing houses.

This year the income was a lump sum and had to last for one year. A few immediate needs could be met and the balance of forty-two dollars, the aid-indebtedness I had received crossing the Pacific Ocean of was paid off.

Anna liked this idea of living closer to her sister because she could visit periodically.

Late in September Dad Friesen had an idea to visit the World's Fair in Chicago. Shortly before leaving his longtime knee injury flared up and caused pain. He and Mom got as far as Reno, Nevada, where they rented a motel. The pain increased. Having a sleepless night, he finally gave in to Mom's pleading to return. At home his family had to lift him out of the car and carry him to bed. The family realized that he needed more than just rest. We were notified that Dad was in the Modesto hospital and expected surgery. Anna wanted to see her father. So we drove up and entered his room. Tubes were leading out of his mouth and nose. He was conscious but unable to speak. Next day the surgeons discovered Dad had suffered an internal stroke causing all these problems. He expired shortly. The burial was in Reedley cemetery next to his son, John.

This very courageous man was born and grew up in South Russia in the village of Friedensfeld, translated "field of peace," the same place my father was born. After acquiring a family, while Anna still was an infant in 1911, new land developments were in progress in Siberia. With a modest sum of ten thousand rubles, Dad Friesen with his family moved to the region of Omsk. Purchasing two hundred desjatin (approximately six hundred acres), he farmed and developed a successful venture. From 1919 with the establishment of Communism, things started to slide down hill until it was futile to continue any longer to live in Russia. Religious freedom and private ownership were in serious jeopardy. Many of the Mennonite faith were desperately looking for an escape route. A very large group had accumulated near Moscow and hoped to obtain exit visas. A few got them. This was rumored to other areas and families by the thousands started to sell out and flock to Moscow. Over thirty thousand squatted in tents and makeshift abodes that became a hazard to life and health.

Chapter 61
The Friesen Escape Plan

While still living on his homestead a child was added to the family by the name of Kolja (Nick). Here his wife, also named Anna died. Dad Friesen then married her sister, Margaret, a widow with three children, George, Louise and Nelly Klassen. Together with his oldest two sons, Henry and John and a nephew, Henry Loewen, the son-in-law, Henry Toews, who married the oldest daughter, Elizabeth, and the brother-in-law, John Funk, with wife and son, contemplated and planned their escape route. They would go to the far east and cross the border into China. Things that were saleable were disposed of in the summertime and they left for Blagovechensk. Here the oldest three were urged to make the crossing as soon as the river froze and was passable and than report back. The news came that they arrived safely in Harbin.

Friesen family.

Preparations were made three horses with three sleighs accommodated the entire group. Coming to a suitable crossing spot, little infant Johnny that Elizabeth recently bore, besides a daughter she had, started to cry. Dad suggested we all stop, satisfy the little hungry one, and then proceed. While the mother fed the little one, Abe, the crippled one, sitting in the rear of the sleigh, scanned the horizon including the various trees. There on the tree he spotted a soldier with a machine gun. As if nothing had happened they proceeded. With quite a distance behind them, they made it across the ice safely to the Chinese side.

Arriving in Harbin Dad had no idea how to find his sons. Walking the streets of this large city, he passed a dealership of some farm implements and stopped and looked through the window. Inside men were working. Suddenly Dad spotted his son, John. John looked up and saw Dad standing outside! It was indeed an interesting discovery to find each other in this manner.

The next remarkable incident when dad found his old friend Dr. Isaak, an eye specialist from Omsk, now practicing here in Harbin. Relating to his friend the concern to get to Canada or the United States, the Doctor said, "I treat the families of most of the foreign consulates and attaches. Let me introduce you to them and you explain the concerns to them directly."

Combined Friesen family.

Dad contacted the Canadian representative first who flatly refused any emigrants from the orient. Next was the American who listened to the Russian refugees and then requested Dad to write the reasons that caused him to flee and seek refuge elsewhere. This is how every detail was put on paper.

The consul sent Dad's testimony to President Hoover, he took it to the Congress and together they voted to admit the accumulated two hundred fifty persons to the United States. All came over except his son, Abe, who couldn't because he was crippled.

Since so many of the refugees were in some kind of financial need to pay for the passage, Dad and Dr.Isaak's youngest brother James, ventured first for the U.S.A. and made their way to Kansas. There they contacted influential officials of the Mennonite Aid and obtained a loan of one hundred twenty dollars for each one who needed it. In later years Anna used these experiences as her testimony. She thought very highly of her father and family.

While in Harbin, China, and waiting for their passports,the refugees wrote home to their relatives about current happenings that they were having about the permits to get to the U.S.A. People from all corners of the Soviet Union started to flock into China, some over the Himalayas. Some in the summertime swam across the Amur river. Some did not make it because of hardships. Others were apprehended and returned. A crowd of over three thousand had accumulated. Their entry to the U.S. was denied. The Mennonite Central Committee took over the plight of those stranded in China and moved them all to South America.

Chapter 62
Family Progress

Another addition came to our family on April 11, 1935. This time I was present and gave encouragement to my wife. The little fellow did not make a sound but when the obstetrician smacked him on his bottom, he expressed himself in a loud protest and started to breathe normally. We named him John Stanley.

Having lived now over five years in the United States, I was concerned about acquiring my citizenship. Corresponding with reliable witnesses to appear in the Fresno courthouse November 18, 1936, the day of the hearing, a few showed up. Mr. Martens was one of them. Others wrote letters. During the hearing the judge found that there was a gap not covered by the letters because of our frequent changing of residency. When the judge hesitated, Mr. Martens spoke up and said, "Your honor, I have known this person and his where abouts from his arrival to this very day and about and I vouch for him."

This covered the needed requirements and I was pronounced a citizen of the United States of America.I was grateful to God and thankful to friends in this hour of need.

By way of explanation the spelling of my name from Tielman to Thielmann was granted at this time. The Russian alphabet does not have the letter "H", so I spelled my name Thielmann. Stumbling on grandfather's records I discovered he spelled our name with an "H" and two n's. The judge agreed to correct the spelling.

In May, 1937 a work position opened in the R.G. Le Tourneau factory in Stockton. They were manufacturing heavy earth-moving equipment. We moved to Stockton. Within six months union agitators caused labor unrest and the plant was closed. Everything was moved to Peoria, Ill. We decided to stay in California.

Close to the end of the year, we moved back to Reedley. After looking around for opportunities for work, an elderly gentleman from the church offered me an acre lot to buy from a parcel of land he had subdivided. For only ninety dollars I had my choice from six lots. I would pay fifteen dollars per month. After thinking this over, we decided in favor of this bargain.

First house I built in Reedley.

Since Pastor Hubert was also operating a lumber yard in a nearby town, consultation with him led to a loan in building materials for the construction of a small house. A good neighbor across the street, familiar with plans and carpentry, assisted in drawing up plans and giving helpful hints where needed.

Single-handedly our project got under way. Every opportunity I had to earn something would mean the project would rest. A little at a time the house was enclosed but not finished. Our moving in into an incomplete dwelling created hardship on my wife with two little children. All water had to be hand-carried in from the neighbor's. The construction noise was not too entertaining.

One afternoon having just sharpened my hatchet for trimming some ends on the gable of the roof, the hatchet slipped and hit my forearm of the left hand and severed an artery. The blood gushed like a fountain. Scared, I ran down the ladder spraying the walls red. It happened at this moment that a neighbor came and took me to the emergency of the local doctor. The nurse put a tourniquet on the arm to stop the bleeding. Next she had to page the physician who was somewhere on house calls. In about an hour the doctor showed up. In the meantime the nurse released the tourniquet periodically. A few stitches with application of antibiotic and I could go home. The next day I resumed where I had left off, only this time with caution.

Eventually the dwelling got finished. A well was drilled and I rigged up a pressure system that supplied domestic water. A cow came in to possession. An electric fence kept the cow confined to the restricted grazing area. Now the family had milk.

In the meantime I continued with the spiritual extension ministry in a nearby small town that did not have a separate building. Since school trustees were involved, the local elementary public school classroom was used as a meeting place. One evening while speaking facing the audience, something flared up outside and caught my attention. One look and I shouted, "Fire!" The trustees looked out the window and then ran outside and put the fire out with a fire extinguisher before it got out of control. The painters that week were using rags and had thrown them into the trash bin that caused spontaneous combustion.

The school board tried to fix the blame on our activities on Sunday. The real facts were that we were the ones that saved this structure by nipping the fire in the bud!

The Department of Interior had a project going to harness the San Joaquin river beyond Clovis. A dam was under construction. Working as a carpenter, the distance going home was too far. So I utilized the contractor's barracks and slept there four nights a week. Saturdays and Sundays were off and I could perform necessary home projects.

In May of 1938 Anna received her citizenship. She was very delighted when the judge commended her for being a house wife, mother of two little children, and going to night school to brush up on the United States Constitution.

The war in Europe caused a great deal of concern to every one. Defense projects sprang up suddenly everywhere. We were pulled off the dam project and assigned to strategic coastal areas to fortify factories and airfield installations.

January 11, 1940 we had another addition in the family. We named him Bruno Henry. When he started to go to school later, he changed it to Henry B.

The following year our son, Johnny, had the measles. In addition to an ear ache, an abscess bothered him. In the hospital the doctor opened it for drainage. Instead of getting better it got worse. The doctor informed us that the boy had sustained a damaged heart. He warned us that the heart was so frail and weak he doubted that the child ever would reach the age of eighteen, twenty never.

With this prognosis we requested the church to pray for our son's recovery. Pastor Hubert and one deacon came and anointed our son with oil and prayed for healing. Johnny got well so he could attend school. The doctor stuck to his prognosis.

Chapter 63
A Business Venture

While working on the air force base in Fresno, I studied books on how to obtain a contractor's license and the knowledge of conducting my own business.

A buyer for our house came around and, considering the deal, we sold it. Then we went to Fresno and bought a suitable lot for our future home.

In the meantime my services at the base were terminated. Because I had time on my hands, Anna desired to visit her Uncle John and Aunt Susie who were living now in San Jose. The first comment Anna made was that it was so much cooler there in San Jose than Reedley. Why not buy a house here? A real estate person showed us a few homes and we settled on one and made a down payment with the lot we owned in Fresno. Anna's brother Nick Friesen helped move our belongings in one trip.

The contractor's license was obtained prior to leaving for San Jose. The place we now were living in was very suitable for my undertaking. Lots were available next to this small subdivision.

No sooner had we got squared away with all the needed requirements of settling after moving, when a letter from the draft board arrived. The information it contained was to report for a medical check up in San Francisco. The answer came back that I had passed and to report on a given date.

Anna had decided that she would invite her stepmother to come and live with her while I was gone. For this reason I closed in an open porch in the rear of the house.

Letters were written to the appropriate branches of service, if there were openings as chaplain. The report was negative. Days of planning, preparation, and anxiety lay ahead. Anna did not know how to operate an automobile. Time was too short to teach her. Many other things were discussed. Just three days before induction, V.J. Day was proclaimed and the whole thing was cancelled. What a relief! Thank God, the bloodshed came to an end.

The post war area brought about the explosion of building homes. Because of rising prices, the government established a controlling office that regulated the sale of homes and named it the O.P.A. Plans had to be submitted and, according to footage, the sale price established.

The rising cost of materials and labor and the frozen products created a gross imbalance. Difficulties for builders and real estate brokers were immeasurable. These were the reasons that the O.P.A. had to be abolished. Now the race had no limit between labor materials and the sale price.

Meeting people in business, I found some men of real attractive character. This is how I discovered the Christian Business Men's Committee, The organization was formed during the Depression in 1933, I joined it.

One afternoon an elderly gentleman with a pickup and horse trailer stopped at one of my projects and asked it he could give me an estimate to put in a front lawn. I consented. He stepped off the the square footage, pulled out his pad and quoted the price. After accepting his bid, he asked if I were a Christian. I confirmed it. He then continued, "We could use you in our local prison witnessing and talking to the inmates."

This was how I became involved in this ministry for twenty-two years, one day a week.

Our children were attending school in their grade levels. Anna started to do some sewing for others which kept her occupied when not performing some house duties. Occasionally relatives visited us which made her happy.

Chapter 64
After War News

After the war newspapers carried some of my relatives' names stranded in the Allied sectors of Germany. They were in gross need. The care organization, was sending out relief packages for ten dollars each. I found ten names on that list. To each one a package was mailed. Horrible experiences started to unfold as news leaked through letters from relatives.

Brother Henry's family.

My brother Henry, two years younger, also was stranded in the Russian zone with his family, but was forcibly returned to the Soviet Union. Now letters started to come,

In the first letter he described the following: he had married a girl from a family I knew. Shortly thereafter he was exiled to Siberia and put to work in the coal mines. For two years he never saw the sunlight. Because of inadequate food, his lungs developed tuberculosis. The prognosis was incurable and they released him to die at home.

Without money or food supplies, he begged his way through from Siberia to the Ukraine. Arriving at home was extremely exhilarating. Through prayers for healing, his health returned.

All correspondence from the Soviet Union had to be sent via Canada because of the strained relationship between ours and their governments. Relatives in Canada started to send dry goods and food packages to those in that country. But from here, there was absolutely no possibility to send either letters or packages. We mailed everything through the relatives in Canada.

Another letter from Mother arrived describing the situation they were in and informing me that Sister Katja had given birth to a daughter. They named her Olga. Sister Katja's husband attended the delivery and then together with Step dad and other men were removed and were never again heard from them nor their where abouts.

Mother in exile with her daughter with daughter and step-daughter.

In 1947 the first Gideon camp in San Jose came into existence and we became members. We had regular Saturday prayer meetings. I regularly attended. They also supplied me with necessary Gideon testaments for our prison ministry.

Business in San Jose fluctuated from high to very low during the Korean conflict. The sales slump in the housing market affected me with two unsold dwellings. The creditors put extreme pressure on me for payments and to declare bankruptcy. I refused. One out of thirteen creditors felt like I did. It was worked out that all would wait until the houses were sold. In less than sixty days a sale transpired and the pressure was off.

Often I have wondered why I had these pressures. It felt as if I were in a pressure cooker. I learned how to be sympathetic to the needs of others.

The landscape contractor who introduced me to the local prison ministry had a heavy cross to bear. His wife's mental condition started to deteriorate and it did not dawn on him that it could be some mental sickness that we have named Alzheimer's disease. She required constant care that he could not provide. Their daughter took her and cared for her. A year later while pulling a power pole he got hit on the head and was physically seriously impaired. He soon disqualified himself and retired.

The condemned, unhealthy and antiquated facilities of the old Santa Clara county jail gave room for a new prison on Hedding Street. We were allowed to use the dining room and only those who wanted came and participated. Here we could use our video tools and present Dr. Irvin Moon's film productions, which consisted of God's creation of nature and the human body. The results helped immensely.

The parole officer issued permanent passes with an I.D. photograph. I could come in anytime I wanted. The newspapers usually would identify criminals and the extent of their misdeed. We seldom asked them about their crime. A young medical doctor of Yugoslavian heritage had killed his newly married wife. He had poured muriatic acid over her vital organs and face to punish her for being unfaithful. She died of these injuries. The doctor later repented of taking matters into his own hands. Now his desires were to become a priest. The jury and judge gave him only ten years. There were evidences that this outburst of behavior was provoked. His wife, a former

Anna and John ready to take off.

beauty queen, carried on love affairs with her admirers as if she were not married.

Several church men were interested in helping train boys to become men. It revolved around modeling toy planes. Three of us agreed to purchase a real plane. We learned how to fly and earned our pilot's license. For Scripture memorization and cooperation in the evening class, the boys were given a plane ride. Saturday spring camping was another exciting experience.

Chapter 65
Family Life

A week before the letter from the draft board came, Anna informed me of her fourth pregnancy. Quick plans were formulated. We would have Stepmother come and attend to Anna's need during my absence. That's why the porch would come in handy. Now since the war had ended, business went on as usual.

I had finished building two houses in this subdivision. The first one was sold, also the one we lived in, and we moved into the second one. Anna progressively felt worse and yet there were no evidences that she was with child. The family physician, after a thorough check up discovered a tumor that required removal. We prayed about this matter and Anna yielded to the physician's recommendation.

The operation disclosed that Anna had a tubal pregnancy. Somehow her body system terminated this pregnancy and she had carried this dead fetus eighteen months. It was unbelievable but the doctor had to admit it.

All three children attended Franklin Grade School in their respective classes according to their age. The attendance had some implication of bickering and not telling the truth of one another. This I would not tolerate and punished the guilty one.

Campbell High School attendance required transportation. Daughter Anna was the first of the children to acquire her driver's license.

In the mean time we had acquired a 1947 Dodge sedan for family use. On school days daughter Anna used it as transportation to drive herself and Johnny to school.

On one of these mornings driving to school, she accidentally hit another student's car in the rear. He filed damages in small claims court. Because Anna was under age, I had to appear together with her. When our case was called, the other party had not appeared. The judge dismissed this case.

Saturdays were the only days we could take care of family needs like shopping and taking vehicles to the garage for service. The Dodge needed lubrication. Johnny was the only one available. I instructed him to follow behind me in the pickup I was driving. After the lube job was done, we proceeded home. Crossing the main street, the traffic officer stopped him.

Watching the happenings in my rear mirror, I immediately stopped and walked back to the scene. The officer questioned him, and he told him, "There is my Dad coming."

I explained to the officer that no one at this time was available and this had to be done. Since Johnny appeared small in the driver's seat, the officer suggested we fix some padding for him to sit on and have a normal driver's look. Arriving at home the son went to work and made up some sort of pad to elevate his appearance.

Chapter 66
Family Changes

Family in San Jose.

Daughter Anna married Wil Rose, a young man, from the First Baptist Church where we were members. After his discharge from the Marines, they settled in Los Angeles area. Here Wil was employed by Dr. Irvin Moon, the producer of Moody films.

While working on the film called, "Red River of Life," Dr. Moon searched for a young mother with a newborn child. Anna Rose and her newborn daughter, Sharon, fit this description. They modeled successfully.

In this film, "Red River of Life," Dr. Moon features the human heart, its functions, and the life sustaining blood from the Creators viewpoint. This marvel organ, the

Daughter Anna with first child.

heart pumps more then three thousand gallons every 24 hours without stopping and also sustains itself. In 1973 Anna and I were visiting the World's Fair in Spokane, Wa. The Moody Institute of Science pavilion showed the "Red River of Life" film. We were glad to see it. As we walked in, a group of ladies had a discussion about some features of the making of the film. Anna joined them and mentioned that we were the parents to the actress who was being shown that night. It stirred quite a bit of interest after the announcer made this public.

From southern California the children moved to Palo Alto. Here another child made an appearance, a son by the name of Dan. From Palo Alto the children moved to Los Altos, where they resided for a number of years. Purchasing an old Cadillac still in good running condition, they were ready to visit some of their friends in Los Angeles area.

Son Dan with family. Now a major in the Airforce.

On that particular morning as Wil got ready to back out of the garage. Dan, eleven years of age, hopped on the rear bumper, sat down, and started to walk while sitting. When the vehicle reached the street the fully loaded car bounced and pinned Dan's foot under the bumper and dislodged him. As Wil opened the door, he noticed Dan under the runningboard. Shocked, he pulled his son from under the car and saw the damage done to his head.

Hastily Dan was rushed to the hospital. After examination the doctors found the left rear wheel had passed over Dan's jaw, face and head, left heavy tire marks and the broken jaw had reset itself. After several days in the hospital and a few weeks at home, the mutilated face had healed. Dan was as good as before. Needles to say this incident cancelled out the trip to the South.

Son John

Son John with family.

Son Johnny at age 18 with his friends, had decided to go to Biola. Having been there little over two years he came home with an excuse for quitting. He was so restless. Talking to the teachers about this, they suggested to quit, do his thing, and when settled, to return.

Looking for a job, he finally enlisted in the Air Force. After training he was sent to Germany. Coming home after his discharge from his tour of duty, he married a local girl by the name of Sandy Larsen. They had four boys, Steve, Dave, Jeff and Jim. Anna loved to baby-sit mostly when Sandy was working.

Occupied with the children, Anna rehearsed Bible Stories

especially, Noah with the animals in the Ark. When Sandy delivered them in the morning, before going to work, they greeted Grandma with the request, "Tell us the story of the Animals in the Ark." They never got tired of that story.

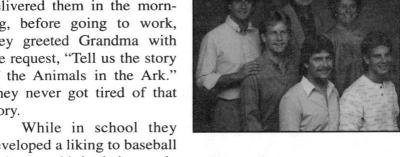

While in school they developed a liking to baseball and pursued it in their growing years.

Johnny worked for the Santa Clara County sheriff's department. After thirty years with them he retired.

Steve, the oldest son, a Certified Public Accountant, is associated with an Accounting office and is busy mostly with Income Tax work.

David, is a fireman and works for the fire department in a nearby city. He is the only one married in this family. They have a daughter and one son.

Jeff is an airline captain and works out of Hawaii. Occasionally he comes home and we get to see him once in a while.

Jim graduated from a law school, passed the bar and is a full fledged attorney. While studying he washed windows for tuition and his livelihood.

Son Henry

Henry was a slow learner. Quite often when he needed help I was not available. One morning he was slow in getting ready for school. He complained of a headache, did not eat his breakfast and felt nauseated. I had a suspicion it could be his appendix that might cause him this discomfort. After he turned on his back I gently pressed in the era of the appendix. He groaned.

I called the doctor and relayed to him my finding. He ordered to take the son immediately to the hospital and he would be there promptly. Surgery revealed a very diseased organ and it was removed promptly. In a few days Henry resumed again school attendance.

In the summertime both sons helped in construction when

Son Henry with family.

needed.

Moody Bible Institute of Chicago featured an aviation course with which Henry was intrigued. After graduating from high school, he left for Chicago. Failing to qualify for this course he came home, after being there a little over two years. While at the Institute Henry met a young lady by the name of Rita. They married and had three sons. Quite often Anna took care of these little brothers.

Chapter 67
Cause To Relocate

In 1963 I successfully bid to construct a residence for a physician employed at Stanford Hospital. The lot being on Stanford property, the owner and architect were present to pinpoint the exact boundaries. Looking at the plans, the owner asked my opinion about the critical span where a wooden beam was designated. I told them, "A steel beam would not sag, a wood beam could."

The construction proceeded as per plans and specifications. Just before the closing in of the frame, the architect requested an additional beam smaller in size to be bolted to it. While filing notice of completion, an obvious sag of this critical area occurred. This was reason for not giving me my final payment. In meantime I had finished another residence with the same architect supervising. The architect would not release the funds of the second job either. Exercising my legal rights, it took two full years before the court awarded me the outstanding funds.

For not paying on our residence, the loan Company foreclosed. Anna and I debated about the cost of redeeming or to just let go of our house. Since a friend from Santa Rosa had invited me to come and build in their newly developed area, we went to look at it. Having had business dealings with him before, we liked what we had seen. On March 1966 we moved to Santa Rosa. Henry with family followed us. Another contributing factor was that I had a contract to build in Lower Lake. The move to Santa Rosa would reduce the mileage.

Chapter 68

Santa Rosa

Relinquishing our property in San Jose without protest, we maintained a good credit with the loan company. It helped us to establish in this new area.

House in Santa Rosa.

Settling down in temporary duplexes, I started the project in Lower Lake. The 60 miles distance over mountain terrain took more than an hour each way. The contract was completed in less than 120 days.

After the completion of the Lower Lake project, Henry and Rita were traveling for weeks at a time. Anna enjoyed taking care of their three sons.

On one morning Anna noticed Michael was somewhat depressed. She asked him, "What's wrong, Michael?" He started to cry and said, "I heard a bad word at school and cannot forget it. I know it is sin." Anna then said, "Let's go see Grandpa, he may have a solution!"

Working down stairs in my shop, I heard the door open. There stood Anna and Michael with tears in his eyes. Switching off the table saw, I faced them. Anna said, "Michael wants to talk to you," and left him standing there. She went back to the kitchen.

The eight year old boy repeated to me the above mentioned problem and now looked up for a solution.

I explained to Michael, "Your young mind is like an empty cup with a few words in it. We are going to put good into it that will teach you how to replace bad words. Will you cooperate with me?" He nodded his head. "Then we will start at lunch time." Some what relieved, he went upstairs.

When I came up for lunch the three boys were already seated at the table. Picking up the Bible I read Psalm 1. "These are the words I want you to memorize! Would you do it?" Michael said, "Yes." Then I looked to Robert and John Mark and repeated the question. They both shook their heads negatively.

For the next six days I drilled Michael both noon and at dinner time. Now I asked him to recite it. No sooner were the words spoken, Robert raised his hand and said, "Grandpa, may I say it?" I permitted it. He rehearsed it flawlessly. After Michael had said it, I asked him, "How do you feel now?" He said, "Better Grandpa." The challenge was made to keep this Psalm always in mind.

In the meantime I purchased a lot in this Wikiup subdivision, drew up a suitable house plan, and started to build our own house. Small repair contracts started to come in which added to our cash flow. After the completion of our residence, I had numerous opportunities to build for others.

The association with the Gideons and the Christian Business Men helped to form binding friendships. It was a pleasure to look forward to each gathering.

At one of our Sunday morning worship service a visiting couple introduced themselves as Dr. Richard and Margaret Getske. Seeing the Gideon emblem on the lapel of my suit, he said, "I wanted to meet a Gideon for some time." I invited them to our various activities.

Retired from the Navy with the rank of a captain, he made inquiry as to the healthiest climate in California. The Navy recommended "Oakmont," near Santa Rosa, where they settled down. Dr. Getske graduated with a Ph.D. in mathematics. He was the originator of the R.O.T.C. programs in the colleges. What he could not figure out he did not accept. In plain words he was an agnostic. Margaret had joined a women's prayer group in a local church around Washington D.C. The group regularly prayed for various needs and also for her husband, Dick.

On a particular day, Dick had an assignment to fly to Anchorage, Alaska. His flight was booked on a regular passenger airline. When the captain called in for the weather he got the go ahead signal. Approaching Anchorage, the captain was advised to return as the airport was covered with solid fog.

"We do not have enough fuel to reach another landing field," the captain replied. Having no other choice but to circle the airport and wait, perhaps the fog might lift before the fuel is exhausted.

After circling numerous times, the captain requested prayer from the passengers. "We only have fuel for one more round, we must land!"

Dr. Richard Getske never prayed. Now he had to decide if

praying to God helps. He bowed and earnestly pleaded for God to save him. When the plane lined up with the runway, a small window opened in the fog and the runway was visible. As soon as the wheels touched the pavement, the sky closed. Dick went to the telephone and called Margaret and related this incident to her. Overjoyed she praised the Lord for saving her husband and having him become a believer in God.

In Santa Rosa the monthly meetings of the Gideons were held in the homes of individual members. Meeting at he home of Dr. and Mrs. Getske, Dick requested special prayer. Washington had given him a special invitation to organize the R.O.T.C. programs in Turkey. This special assignment would be for two years. The Getskes desired the Lord's leading in this matter. At the close of the meeting I asked Dick, "Suppose you have a heart attack. Where would you find help?"

Sometime later in the week, Dick related, they had decided not to accept the assignment.

A few months later Dick was in the intensive care unit of the hospital. The doctors had diagnosed that the arteries on each side of his neck were clogged. The lack of blood to the brain had triggered a heart attack. After the surgery, he was on his feet again.

One rainy Wednesday evening after a prayer meeting, all had gone home except Dick and a retired pastor with his wife. Visiting for sometime the rain let up and they proceeded to their automobiles. Here Dick asked the pastor for the key to unlock the door. The pastor fumbled in his pocket without producing the keys. Dick got a flashlight from his car and pointed toward the ignition. There were the keys! Dick had a new Cadillac and the pastor drove an older model Pontiac. Both were made by General Motors. A telephone was not available at this time of the night to call the AAA truck for assistance. Dick now prayed.Perhaps his key would do the trick. Putting the Cadillac key into the Pontiac door handle, the door opened.

After the pastor and his wife were seated inside the car, Dick wanted to know for sure if the key really worked. After the doors were locked, he tried again first one side, the key didn't work. Now the other side and it also did not work. Then he tried the ignition, the same results. This was another confirmation that the Lord answers prayers. The Lord moves in a mysterious way His wonders to perform!

Chapter 69
Anniversary

While still in San Jose, a few friends were invited to our house to celebrate our 25th wedding anniversary, December 27th, 1957. The children were not present except Henry. We rejoiced with friends and the program they prepared. It cheered all of our hearts.

Our 50th wedding celebration was in Santa Rosa at the church we attended. All three children with their families were present. Friends had prepared an evening dinner with a beautiful program that followed. Nick and Helen Friesen, Anna's brother, also had come from Reedley. He surprised us with a poem engraved on a metal plaque. Grandson Dan read it:

John & Anna Thielmann

While the clouds of revolution gathered
On the horizon of that distant land,
John and Anna joined their fleeing families
Fleeing, fleeing like a Gypsy band.

Though they did not know each other
On those Russian plains so far away,
They escaped by way of China,
Bound to meet in Reedley some great day.

The leading in their lives defies description,
How the Master up in Heaven above
Guided them on land and sea and ocean
And then to meet and fall in love.

John once lived with her good brothers,
All five of them in bachelor state,
In their need they hired this young lady
Who was to cook and thus relieve their fate.

T'was then the sparks began to flourish,
Love began to find its rightful place,
John could not control his own emotions
As he gazed upon her lovely face.

Then one day he broke the barrier
And proposed a marriage plan,
To this kind and blushing tender maiden
Who was looking for a Christian man.

She, the beauty queen of our family,
He, the pride of all the Thielmann clan,
Joined their hands in Reedley, California,
Blending life and love according to God's plan.

Both had learned to love their precious Savior,
Both had longed to serve their Lord,
So they had a blessed loving family
Based and founded on God's Word.

First appeared a lovely daughter,
She must bear her mother's name,
Then came John and then came Henry,
Destined for their share of joy and fame.

Now there is no greater joy or blessing
On this 50th anniversary
Than to hear your friends and children
Talk about your life of faith and victory.

Just to know that you've succeeded
As you longed to lend a helping hand,
You have made this life more pleasant
For the pilgrimage in this land.

So we stop to praise the Master
For His mercy that has kept you day by day,
Keep your faith and trust in Jesus,
He will lead and safely guide you all the way.

Chapter 70
Unpleasant Surprise

After finishing up a remodeling job, I was resting in the middle of the week. For an unknown reason my stomach and chest felt very uncomfortable. I asked Anna what I had eaten that my stomach felt pain. Same as usual she told me. No matter what position I rested, sitting, walking, or standing, the painful feeling would not leave me. Sunday morning I called the family physician. The substitute doctor asked about how long I had the feelings. I told him it had been three days. Then he stated, "You do not have a heart attack; see your doctor Monday."

Next day I drove to our family physician. Checking my pulse and listening to the heart, he abruptly asked, "How do, you want to be driven to the hospital? Shall I call an ambulance or may I drive you?"

"I will drive by myself," I replied.

"Under no circumstances can you drive," was his statement. The doctor drove me to the emergency and wheeled me in.

Placed in the intensive care room I nearly passed out. Appropriate heart medication and treatments were administered. After ten days I was released. The doctor prescribed a heart medicine that I still adhere to.

Anna had foot surgery, first in her left one. After several months, the right foot also underwent the same treatment.

Sitting in the chair was not my habit. Having all the needed wood cutting tools, my time was mostly spent in building furniture. Beautiful curios were designed and made. Anna liked them. She suggested to make one for each child and surprise them. While working in the garage after the first week of Anna's second surgery, I injured my left index finger. Accidentally it slipped into the rotating circular saw blade. Since I was unable to handle the dishes, Anna got up and did them. This early walking prevented the foot from proper healing. It hurt her from this time on.

Anna Has Cancer

A routine physical checkup disclosed Anna had cancer in the uterus. What a shock! Upon the recommendation of our physician, the surgery was performed at the U.C. hospital. The acting surgeon remarked that he had removed all malignant tissue. After a monthly checkup the cancer had spread. The only treatment that could check this type of cancer was radiation.

Thirteen radiation treatments were administered without checking this cancer. Anna had made up her mind that this is the end. I persuaded her to try chemotherapy to which she finally yielded.

The undesirable end result disappointed us. She lost all hair, lost her appetite, and had a sore mouth and throat. Eating and swallowing was painful. In spite of what the oncologist suggested to coax Anna to eat, it did not work. She sat at the table and cried.

Two weeks prior a friend of Anna's had sent a testimony of a registered nurse on tape about how she had recovered from cancer by eating Barleygreen. I lost no time and sent for a sample of this product. I mixed Anna a drink as soon as the product had arrived. Regardless of pain, she managed to swallow some of it. Within one week Anna's mouth had healed that she could eat a normal meal. We showed the Dr. the literature of this product. After one month the cat-scan proved positive results and chemotherapy was suspended. Both of us were using Barleygreen with beneficial results. Friends were now asking what we were using that Anna's health has improved. Upon the discovery of these benefits, we had many customers with equal health results.

Since all of our children were living in Mountain View and the San Jose area, we decided to follow the advice of our physician and to move closer to them. We put our house up for sale.

Visiting daughter Anna one day, she suggested to look at her rental house that we could remodel if we wanted. It looked attractive to us and, with some addition and changes, it was a good proposition. We accepted it.

Chapter 71
Mountain View

Before June of 1988 the escrow of the sale of our house closed. The children and friends helped us move all our belongings to Mountain View. With the knowledge that we planned to remodel, things were stored in the garage.

We wasted no time. Plans were drawn, permit taken out, and work started as soon as approval from the planning commission arrived. This addition kept me busy the balance of the year. Son Henry and friends lent a helping hand when needed. Mostly Anna and I were the construction crew. Remodeling the kitchen with new self made cabinets and appliances to suit Anna was delightful.

It was a great pleasure to make acquaintance with the local Gideons and to participate. We liked the singing and preaching in the First Baptist Church of Los Altos which we also joined as members. The close proximity of the children enlivened our life here. We got to see and share with them more often.

October 17th, 1989, at 5:00p.m., I sat in the new addition at the bar, admiring my handiwork in the kitchen. A sudden violent house movement made me wonder if the building would stand up. Anna had the vacuum cleaner going and did not hear the noise. Feeling the motion and then my shouting, she stopped. The building sustained no damage. This earthquake had done considerable damage in the cities of San Francisco and Oakland.

Our move compelled me to look for a new cardiologist and for Anna an oncologist. I felt great, Anna's monthly visits to the doctor still were negative. One morning getting up she pointed to her left ankle and showed me a large black mole. Immediately I made an appointment with the doctor. After an examination by a pathologist, the horrible word Melanoma cancer was uttered.

Surgery removed approximately three inches of her surface skin and required skin grafting. The oncologist also put Anna on an austere, expensive chemical treatment. The prognosis showed probable additional surgeries on the lymph glands.

Daughter Anna and friends recommended we do some traveling and take our minds off this illness. They all pooled their money and bought us tickets to fly to Germany.

Chapter 72
A Delightful Visit

We lived through a delightful experience in 1979. My brother, Henry, with family had arrived in Bremen, Germany in 1978 from Russia. I had not seen him since 1929 when he still was single. Now Anna also met him and his family. At the same time we also partook of the Gideon convention in Germany. We stayed there a whole month.

Visiting in Germany.

Sister Katja with daughter, Olga, had arrived from Russia in June of 1990. I had not seen Sister for sixty-one years, We promised to come and visit her.

The last part of August we arrived in Frankfurt, Germany. The nephews, Gerhard and Ernst, came and picked us up and drove us to Bremen. It was near midnight when we arrived at Ernst's place where all had assembled. A hearty welcome was extended. We did not stay up too long.

The following days were filled with meeting the family members and getting acquainted. After all the commotion was over, I wanted to know more about their life style in the Soviet Union.

Sister now filled in the questions I had of the horrible experiences they went through in the concentration camps in the Soviet Union.

These were once in a lifetime wonderful experiences; to visit relatives we had never met and a sister we had not seen for 61 years! The Lord had provided. We have been so grateful for that vacation.

We did not meet brother Henry's daughter and family and his youngest son with family on our first visit. They had not arrived yet from Russia. The oldest son now also had a family. We met them all.

The third week in Germany, Anna pointed to a tender feeling in her left groin area. We left it up to the oncologist to find out what it could be. The foot grafting had healed. The donor skin area had almost healed. Visiting, conversation, and traveling distracted Anna's mind from being too preoccupied with herself and future probabilities.

Last minute information to glean from Sister's memory about their life style and experiences was painful for her. They were so glad to be in their present environment. There are no words to describe the pain and sufferings of the innocent in the concentration camps they have been in. The lack of food and how they managed to survive on poisonous mushrooms, was incredible. I asked her what they had done to the mushrooms to make them edible.

The secret that mushrooms were first cooked, then the first water was discarded. Fresh water was added, they were recooked, and then they were eaten. This had made them harmless.

I asked further questions, "What about Step Dad, your husband, stepsister Adina, and how did mother die?"

Sister Katja was quiet for sometime. Then she added, "Mother and Adina died a natural death. The men folks were all killed." She added, "For Christ's sake we must forgive."

The rehashing of past experiences, of cruel and inhumane treatments, caused painful emotions. Only the Lord Jesus, Who taught us to love our enemies also supplied the strength to forgive.

Visiting with Brother Henry, his family, sister Katja, and her daughter, brought many memories to the surface. It was a delightful visit indeed. At the same time we also visited other nephews and friends who live scattered in various parts of Germany.

It was an uneventful flight from Frankfurt to San Francisco. Almost ten hours of sitting still tried my patience to the limit. We were glad we came home in one piece.

Chapter 73
Surgery and Departure

Shortly before Anna's Passing.

After resting a few days, Anna paid the surgeon a visit who promptly scheduled surgery. Instead of one lymph node, two were removed in the groin area. He suggested for Anna to come back in one week to remove the stitches. A week later, the day following the removal of the stitches, Anna wanted to dress the wound. To her dismay she saw an open gap. I looked at it and called the doctor. In his office I asked the doctor, "How come the wound has not healed?"

The answer came, "Radiation has killed the skin." To the former statement I replied, "Then radiation caused this cancer." The doctor did not reply.

Although the wound gradually narrowed, Anna's general condition deteriorated. The oncologist discovered that the liver also was affected. He gave up all treatment and suggested to have a hospital bed in the home and nurses come and care for Anna.

A bed was installed in the dining room accessible also to visitors. From the Visiting Nurses Association, we received quality care. The oncologist supplied us with needed pain-killing drugs and I administered them as needed. A two-way monitor was set up from Anna's bed to mine. Any time at night she needed something, I would get up and attend to it.

Still alert and having the presence of her faculties, she talked to the nurses about her experiences. As a member of the Gideon Auxiliary, Anna presented each ministering nurse with one of the white New Testaments and pointed out the helps section. On one of these occasions the head nurse remarked, "I have another patient that is fearful and restless. I'll present her with this Testament."

A week later as the same nurse ministered to Anna, she

remarked, "I gave the Testament to the lady that was so fearful of dying and pointed out where to find help. The following time when I returned, she was not afraid anymore."

My patient became weaker by the day. When hearing the extra groaning at night, I would get up and tend to whatever need Anna had. Death was anticipated. The Nurses Association left literature describing signs of the last minutes of someone who was dying.

On November 6th, her temperature went up beyond normal, the pulse raced, I went to the phone and called the children. Daughter Anna and a friend responded, the others could not make it. We all knelt at mother's bed on each side. Prayer of release and thanks for mother's life and testimony was offered. Psalm 116:15, "Precious in the sight of the Lord is the death of His saints." We were married 59 years, 10 months and 9 days.

An open casket memorial service was held at the funeral parlor. Burial followed at the Alta Mesa cemetery. A simple marker with both of our names on it decorates the grave site.

The many weeks of vigil, both day and night,exhausted my emotions. After everything had been settled, I gradually started to unwind. Undescribable and difficult weeks followed. The Lord gave grace to make the adjustment. All the house work, cooking, baking, laundering, and cleaning, I learned.

A few months later the children and friends helped to have a garage sale. Things that I could get along without were sold. Some household items were already designated to each child in mother's lifetime. They would receive these things after my passing.

Chapter 74

Dr. John Isaak

Never had I heard of this gentleman until I came to Harbin. Dad Friesen's family related the matter regarding refugees pointing out Dr. Isaak as the key person in our relocation.

As an eye specialist and a very sought after physician, Dr. Isaak treated all the families of the foreign attache's besides the general public. Prior to coming to Harbin, Dad Friesen knew Dr. Isaak from the city of Omsk, where he operated his own hospital.

With anticipation Dad looked forward to the renewal of friendship with this old friend, relating to him the desires to emigrate to Canada or the U.S.A. Upon this the doctor said, "I am acquainted with the gentlemen that represent these countries. I'll speak to them regarding this matter."

Dr. Isaak spoke to the Canadian consul who flatly refused to talk about this case. His country did not admit anyone from China.

Next the doctor approached the American consul, who with interest listened and then requested Dad to furnish his reasons for leaving Russia. With great detail Dad wrote his story and handed it in. After translating it into English, the consul forwarded the story to President Hoover.

After the immigration permit to America was granted, this physician treated all immigrants for physical fitness. When my turn came, I had a conversation with the doctor's sister, who was a nurse in the clinic. Upon seeing my name, Thielmann, she said, "I visited the property where you lived and know your background." This surprised me.

A few years later the doctor sent his two sons to California. Just before the invasion of China by the Japanese army, Dr. and Mrs. Isaak also came to California and settled in Fresno. Here he tried to obtain his doctor's credentials which were denied. This intelligent, kind physician, because of the language barrier, had to start from scratch. Working in the hospital and at the same time learning the language, ended up being too difficult a task. A stroke paralyzed one side and caused him to be bedridden. The family moved to Vallejo.

We were living in San Jose at that time and decided to visit our ailing friend. Anna's uncle, John Funk, with Aunt Susie,

166   *Escape to Freedom*

Anna, and I visited this family to cheer them up. During the conversation he said he was hungry for the old fashioned baked zwieback.

On the way home Anna expressed her desire to bake the above mentioned zwieback. That week she fulfilled her wish. On the following Sunday we again went for a visit and delivered the goodies. Shortly after that incident he passed away. The burial was in Reedley, California.

Mrs. Isaak moved to one of her son's in Petaluma and resided there for a few years. Aging, she became feeble and was cared for in a convalescent place. We visited her periodically and she heartily appreciated this kindness. She died shortly and was buried next to her husband.

A great tribute of gratitude was expressed to Dr.Isaak and Dad Friesen who together facilitated and implemented the immigration of two hundred and fifty refugees into U.S.A. and freedom.

Chapter 75
The Culture and Habits of the Ukraine

The earliest recollection of my contact with Russian nationals was with our baby sitter, a girl named Zenja. She was the oldest daughter of four children of the carpenter that lived across the street. Every morning she helped us boys get dressed. Other times her help was needed in the kitchen. She quickly learned the Dutch language that we spoke in the family.

Martha a more mature and quite older woman, had charge of the kitchen. She was a polite, friendly person, always willing to accommodate our family. She lived in a room next to the kitchen. She was of medium build, about five feet two inches, and had a very disfigured face. I asked Mother one day about Martha's face, whether she was born that way. "Ask her," she said.One day I had the courage and asked her, "Martha, were you born that way?"

She answered, "No! As a small child five years of age, I watched my father do some remodeling in the entry of our house. He was installing a crawl hole between the joist. I stood below and watched the procedure. The ax slipped from his hand and fell squarely across my face with the sharp edge down, cutting between the eyes and the tip of my nose. It healed that way." Periodically she had severe nose bleeding ever since. Martha stayed with us till Grandma had arrived. Then she left for her home in Poltava, several hundred miles north of us.

All native children including those of our employees were attending school in a nearby town ten miles east. The distance was commuted by train morning and evening.

Occasionally I was allowed to enter the homes of our employees with whose children I wanted to play. The outstanding feature of the room decoration of these homes was the corner where religious pictures were displayed of Mary, the Mother of Jesus, and a patron saint. In front suspended from the ceiling hung a small glass dish filled with olive oil and a floating wick lit and burning day and night. Before they left the house,they knelt in front of the pictures and crossed their chest, a religious observance taught by their parents.

The Greek Orthodox Church was the only authorized religious body that was empowered to discipline the citizens. Any dissidents were punished and exiled to Siberia.

The Gregorian calendar, which is fourteen days later than the Roman, was officially observed by the state and the church. Most holidays were meticulously observed, especially Christmas, New Year, Easter, Pentecost and some Saints days. Every village had a church with tall steeples, round cupolas, and a bell. On quiet days we could hear the church bells toll in the far distance.

A few days before Easter, Mother would bake special Easterbread. All the Russian girls anticipated this holiday and Mother would give each one a small bread to take along to church. On Good Friday they fasted all day. Early in the evening they walked in company of other women to their church about five miles away.

The next day I would ask some of the younger girls, "How was it?" They would relate that the priest had blessed the bread and their sins were forgiven and now they could eat. The only complaint they had about the young boys and men that they were always crowding and pressing around the church trying to separate a girl and seduce her.

On Christmas day wellwishers would come in groups of five to ten young men from the village. They had prepared a four foot star out of twigs and covered with parchment transparent paper. It was rotated by hand on a handle with a lit candle inside. Tassels were fastened to the points. As many as could crowd into the entry, did so, and in unison chanted the Christmas greeting to a melody while rotating the star at the same time. When they finished, Mother would send me down with a loaded plate with baked goodies, sometimes also some money. These young men would repeat the same wellwishing in as many homes as they were allowed to enter.

The lady cook that was hired to cook for some single employees had two daughters, one son, and an alcoholic husband. Always on holidays and weekends he was intoxicated. The behavior of this man changed from a normal human being to a beast. On one of these occasions he threw the empty whiskey bottle at his small son with a force that embedded the neck of the bottle in the forehead of his son and left a lifelong scar. Nearly everyone knew how to brew whiskey.

Chapter76

The Deliveries of Produce

Most of the older farmers were illiterate and instead of a signature, they made a cross. After the harvest deliveries were made, some crops were harvested too early and the kernels did not have the proper body nor weight. Some men put rocks and bricks in the bottom of their sacks. The administration was prepared for all of these tricks. To evaluate all these deficiencies, proper tools were acquired and used. Before the grain was weighed the receiver put the metal probe into the sacks. Any hard object was immediately detected. The farmer then was requested to dump the whole content outside for examination. If foreign objects were present, his entire load was rejected. The other farmers laughed, red faced, he showed his extreme embarrassment. It did not take long and the conduct of the farmers improved.

This beautiful land had a rolling surface with occasional valleys. Trees were rare unless planted. When traveling one could see huge mounds of dirt piled up in a pyramid-like shape with rounded tops on the horizon. Some could have been possibly fifty or more feet tall. No one was able to cultivate on them.

Looking out of the two story window one of these hills, (in Russian we said "Mogilla") was visible.I asked my father one day, what was the purpose of those hills?

He answered, "Long before our time there were wars between the Turks and the Kosaks. Whenever a notable leader died, he was buried with his horse, saddle and war paraphernalia."

The one visible from the window had been plowed and grain sown on it. In later years, after father had passed away, I managed the affairs. Quite often when working around this hill, I had a desire to dig in and find out for sure what this was all about. Time never came, other matters were too demanding.

Chapter 77
Domestic and Wildlife

Not every one had horses, but most had oxen. Cows, pigs, sheep and chicken were in abundance. If water was nearby ducks and geese were also in possession. Without dogs and cats a farmer did not feel comfortable. Some had hunting dogs and had excitement by going rabbit or fox hunting.

We had some stray cats that were undesirable. Quite often we boys would point the dogs at them and they chased the cats up a tree. Step dad had seen it one time and then he told us the experience of a farmer he knew.

This particular man wanted excitement. Catching his unwanted tom cat and putting it in a sack was no problem. Summoning his few dogs, he walked to a nearby empty field where there were no trees.

Arriving at a desirable spot, he let go of the top, with the other hand he shook the cat out of the sack. Bewildered the cat made a run into the opposite direction from the dogs but was overtaken. Scared, it returned to the owner and, climbed on top of the farmers' head and with the claws hung on for dear life. Being in pain the man tried to get the cat from his head. The animal would not budge. Being in pain the man groaned and hollered.

Now the dogs got into a frenzy and jumped on the owner to reach the cat and by doing so pushed him to the ground. While on the ground the man had his hands on the cat that would not let go. The dogs now having access to the animal they hated, were pulling it to pieces. Being in this frenzy, they did not distinguish between the cat and the hands of their owner. Badly bitten by his own dogs, and clawed by the cat he came home wounded, humiliated and in a sorry frame of mind.

The warning was clear, never get into this kind of sport.

Among the villagers were some that had small orchards of a variety of fruits. Only trees that could stand the harsh climate were cultivated. Among those were: apples, pears, plums, cherries and walnuts. Some of those farmers were expert horticulturists. Grandfather hired some who planted his orchards.

Chapter 78
Disasters and Accidents

Mother related to me some disasters that happened while I still was a crib baby.

The first flour mill was a wooden structure with limited machinery. It soon caught fire and burned to the ground. The second building was an improved version, part brick and part wood. A few years later, at midnight Father looked out of the window. Flames were visible and coming from the wooden part of the structure. Jumping out of bed with limited clothes on, he ran quickly to the employees' quarters and started to wake the men to come and help douse the fire.

Father must have knocked pretty hard on the doors or windows. One of the employee's child was scared to death. The parents blamed Father for the death of their child. They quit and moved away. The third structure was enlarged and erected completely out of brick except for wooden floors and rafter parts. The roof was metal. This three story building had a new engine and flour machinery to produce the finest flour the market demanded.

The farm had its share of mishaps. Most of the hired seasonal employees came from the province of Poltava. Minor injuries were taken care of by Aunt Emma, the obstetrician. Fatal accidents happened mostly during threshing seasons.

A young woman was hauling sheaves with a team of horses. Sitting on top of the sheaves and being in a hurry, fell forward on the horses which trampled her to death. The other fatality involved a young mechanic. While supervising the operation, he came too close to the driving belt, was drawn in and killed.

Being prejudicially minded, each time something like the above mishap occurred, a group of women would quit and go home. The knowledge of accident prevention was lacking. After serious accidents every one observed safety more carefully.

Chapter 79

Atheism

A drastic change came over the the whole land when the government introduced the idea that there is no God. The state church was no longer in control and was not government supported. An apathy existed. Older folks still clung to their faith. The younger generation was divided. Some went with the new idea. Others sought a deeper spiritual meaning by reading God's Word and experienced a new birth in Christ.

Evangelism was now conducted by their own people. Many welcomed this freedom and accepted Christ by faith as savior. On one occasion, in a nearby village, there were a number of people who desired to be baptized in open water. Because of some opposition from their own village folks, they walked about eight miles nearer our place. This I wanted to witness.

Hitching a team of horses to a wagon, my brother and I drove in that direction to witness this rare occasion. There were approximately thirty people standing at the edge of this small body of water. Getting ready to enter the water, a few men from the nearby houses also approached about a hundred feet distant. There these men undressed in plain view and went naked in and out of the water periodically mocking the baptism.

Realizing the embarrassment on the leader's part, I approached him and suggested he come to our place. They followed my suggestion. Approximately ten people were baptized. The service was conducted with reverence and without interference. The radiant face told the marvelous transformation that occurred in each life.

Religious gatherings were discouraged after I had left. In 1931 they began to arrest believers, preachers, priests, rabbis, educators, and former landowners, and exiled them north into concentration camps, near and around Vologda and other areas. Former medical doctors, and merchants were not excluded. All were classified at undesirables.

One of the letters from Step dad mentioned that "We all cried to one God for deliverance."

Deliverance came from this misery through starvation, freezing to death, or just being killed with a bullet.

Chapter 80

Rats

One Saturday morning I was traveling to Sunnyvale for an appointment. At this early hour, 6:30 a.m., the El Camino Real had light traffic, none coming in the opposite direction. At a distance a cat appeared, crossing the street. A small animal hopped in front of the cat, which turned out to be a rat. The cat looked Siamese, with a long tail. Whenever the cat gained on the rat, it stopped, opened its jaws and stood still. The cat then backed off. The rat proceeded to hop on. The moment the cat gained on the rat, the rat stopped and faced the cat. This procedure continued until the rat reached the curb, climbed up and stood its ground. By now I passed the scene and reasoned that it must be a domesticated cat, perhaps declawed, and never having to fended for it self was the reason it did not fight. This scene brought back a memory I encountered at home in the Ukraine in 1921.

That year we had a crop failure. The granary was swept to recover every bit of grain, except for the grain caught in the cracks and crevices of the floor. Rats had chewed through the wooden floor at the corners and had invaded this building by the dozens. We did not have traps and poisons. I came up with a plan to rid the granary of rats. I would lay a brick at each hole. When I was sure the rats had entered the granary I would run in close the doors and put the bricks over the escape holes cutting off their route of escape.

Next morning I followed up on my plan. I had a flat shovel along to hit as many of the rats as quickly as possible. While in the process of hitting these rats, they scurried along the edge to get away into their holes. Once they found the hole covered and had nowhere to run they stopped and boldly started to come towards me. In spite of this counter attack I prevailed. That was the last we saw of those rats.

We had cats in the barns that fed themselves on mice and other rodents. One day the horses were out and I noticed a cat fighting with a rat. Both were lying on their side, the rat had attached itself to the throat of the cat and the cat was scratching the rat with all four paws. Being repeatedly scratched the rat finally gave up and fled. The cat was badly bitten and bleeding profusely. The instinct of fight or flight was very strong in these rodents and they were formidable opponents for the cats.

Appendix

In retrospect of my physical contact with Communism in the Ukraine and the flight to China, I experienced frequent nightmares. The supplemental information received later through letters from Step dad and Mother describing their horrible state of existence, caused me to be concerned almost day and night.

Knowing that I was absolutely helpless to assist them, I frequently had dreams of visual contact with them. Since the U.S.A. had no relationship with the Soviet Union, it was impossible to write to them direct. Letters had to be sent to relatives in Canada, who then mailed them to Russia.

All these experiences and concerns contributed to my dreams, that at times I became extremely restless and groaned loud at night. Anna then shook me and asked: "What is wrong?" Avoiding conversation at this hour of the night, I related my horror dreams to her at breakfast time.

Anna prayed for me and these night experiences ceased. The question so important in life is; how can two walk together unless they agree. The added feature is that the Lord said, where two or three are gathered in my name, there I am in the midst of them.

I sincerely trust while reading my life story you came to realize that as the Lord is interested in my life He is also interested in your personal life.

The Author.

Bibliography

Letter from Alfred H. Radekopp.
  Winnipeg, Manitoba, Canada.

Mennonite Exodus, by Frank Epp. Chart.

At the Gates of Moscow.

Historical Books

Three-hundred Year Jubilee Reign
  of the House of Rommanofs.
  Stanford, California.

World Atlas, Readers Digest, Map.

King James Bible, Quotations.